Charles Fillmore

Charles Fillmore

Herald of the New Age

Hugh D'Andrade

HARPER & ROW, PUBLISHERS

New York, Evanston, San Francisco, London

Dedicated to
Eric Butterworth

FIRST EDITION

Designed by Janice Stern

Library of Congress Cataloging in Publication Data

D'Andrade, Hugh.
  Charles Fillmore: herald of the new age.

  Bibliography: p.
  1. Fillmore, Charles, 1854–1948. 2. Unity School of Christianity.
BX9890.U5D36   289.9 [B]   73–6337
ISBN 0–06–061682–2

Contents

Acknowledgments

This book has been enriched by the kindness and interest of many of the staff workers and executives at Unity headquarters. In my interviews with them it turned out that I had an experience which does not often fall to the lot of a writer on religious subjects. Though the subject matter was vital to those I interviewed, never once did I receive the slightest hint regarding what I should write—or should not write.

No slightest attempt was made to guide my thinking or to channel my thought processes, implicitly or explicitly, directly or indirectly. There was not the least suggestion of censorship, nor was there any request to review my manuscript. Of course I submitted my manuscript to those whom I interviewed as a proper courtesy, but here again, except for changing a word or two of dialogue, or correcting an error of fact, no other suggestions were made.

My gratitude goes to:

Eric Butterworth, minister of the Unity Center of Practical Christianity, New York City. He is a second-generation Unity minister, his mother having been a Unity minister in the early days of the movement. He began his service in Silent Unity, serving under May Rowland. He has served as a minister at Unity Temple in Kansas City, Missouri, at Unity centers in Rockland, Illinois, Pittsburgh, Pennsylvania, and Detroit, Michigan. Radio has been one of his main thrusts, and he is well known as a radio speaker. Every day for the past twenty-five years there has been an Eric Butterworth broadcast on the air. He is the author of several successful inspirational books.

James Dillet Freeman, first vice-president, Unity School of Christianity. He is also the director of Silent Unity. He is the poet laureate of Unity, with a renown that goes far beyond the movement. His poem "I Am There" was carried to the moon by an astronaut in the summer of 1971. James Dillet Freeman is also the dean of Unity's historians. His book *The Household of Faith* contains information from which I have liberally drawn, with his gracious consent. He is the teacher of comparative religion at Unity School. As director of Silent Unity he is also the spiritual research director of the Unity movement. James Dillet Freeman is the author of many inspirational books, and of hundreds of poems.

James A. Decker, editor of Unity and senior editor of the editorial department of Unity School. For many years he has guided the editorial policy of Unity with its many publications. He is the author of several books.

Charles Rickert Fillmore, president, Unity School of Practical Christianity. He is also the director of education and public relations. He is the grandson of Charles and Myrtle Fillmore, his father being Rickert Fillmore. As chief executive of the school he regards his work as a stewardship. With the aid of his executive committee his direction and business acumen determine the course of the Unity School.

Lowell Fillmore, president emeritus of Unity School of Christianity. He is the son of Charles Fillmore. The first editor of *Weekly Unity,* he remained the editor for many years. He has worked in every capacity in Unity, from job-press printer up to general manager. He is the author of several books and poems. Succeeding his father as president, Lowell Fillmore has devoted his whole life to Unity.

Louis E. Meyer, chaplain of Unity School, Unity Village. He has served as a minister at Unity centers in Topeka, Kansas, in Rochester,

New York. In Kansas City he served as minister of the Unity Society of Practical Christianity for twenty-seven years. He has lectured widely throughout the country. He is a prolific author. As chaplain of the Unity School at Unity Village his work of personal ministry is a crowning service to the movement.

Ralph R. Rhea, co-director of the radio and television department of Unity School, former secretary-treasurer of the Unity Minister's Association. He writes the scripts for Unity's television ministry. He has served as a Unity minister in Oklahoma City, Oklahoma, in Miami, Florida, and in Oak Park, Illinois.

Rosemary Fillmore Rhea, co-director of the radio and television department of Unity School. She is the daughter of Rickert Fillmore, granddaughter of Charles Fillmore. She has studied at the Pasadena Playhouse, and has been active for several years in radio and television work. Television is her speciality, and the expansion of television programs for Unity throughout the United States and Canada is her concern.

May Rowland, former vice-president of Unity School of Christianity and director of Silent Unity. May Rowland has devoted her life to Silent Unity, having started her work under Charles Fillmore. She is the author of inspirational Unity books. She spends her time writing and traveling, writing even on her travels. Her articles are important features in *Daily Word* and *Unity.*

Vera Dawson Tait, director of the Correspondence School of Unity, formerly course adviser of the Unity Training School. She is an ordained minister. For many years Vera Dawson Tait has been a lecturer at Unity School, teaching in all the various classes. She has taught and lectured in the United States, Canada, and Europe. Her knowledge of Charles Fillmore's teachings is comprehensive and profound.

Ernest C. Wilson, minister of Unity Temple, Unity-on-the-Plaza, Kansas City. Ernest Wilson is the dean of Unity ministers. In his early work at Unity headquarters under Charles Fillmore, he served as editor of *Youth,* one of the Unity publications, and also as editor-in-chief of Unity publications. Upon Charles Fillmore's retirement from the pulpit of the Kansas City Society of Practical Christianity, Ernest Wilson became his successor. After four years the Rev. Mr. Wilson went to Los Angeles, where he founded Christ Church, Unity. Twenty-seven years later he returned to Unity Temple, Kansas City, as minister. He is the author of many books, magazine articles, and poems.

Prologue

How shall a man be measured, how shall he be known? How measure the immeasurable, how know the unknown? For every man is immeasurable, and within him there is a kingdom unknown.

"By their fruits ye shall know them."

Charles Fillmore, co-founder of Unity with his wife Myrtle Fillmore, may be known in part by his fruits. The world-famous Unity movement, the Unity School of Practical Christianity, and Silent Unity are fruits of Charles Fillmore's life.

A sanctuary of unceasing prayer, Silent Unity, at the heart of Unity Village, is the quintessence of these. Through the window of this sanctuary in a quiet midwestern village light shines day and night, month after month, year after year. Known to countless metaphysical students all around the world, this window of light is a symbol that "someone hears." Whatever the hour, day or night, someone is there to reply to a telephone call; someone always prays for the person needing prayer.

Workers in the prayer room receive a constant stream of telephone calls from all parts of the United States and the world. Two hundred thousand telephone calls flow annually into the room, bringing requests for prayer from people in distress, in pain, in grief, in need, in trouble, in the somber cloud of some dark crisis.

In addition Silent Unity receives seven hundred and fifty thousand letters annually asking for prayer. So prayers pour forth unceasingly day and night for the healing of the sick, for the comfort of the sorrowing, and for the solution of all manner of human problems. Devoted servers work for eight-hour periods in an unbroken chain.

The letters written in gratitude for these prayers tell of ailments cured though they were deemed incurable, of problems solved though they were believed unsolvable. Mail accumulates into such mountains that letters cannot be kept in Unity's files for more than five years. It is not possible to count the millions of people who have been blessed by these prayers since Charles and Myrtle Fillmore established the Society of Silent Help ten years before the dawn of this century.

Workers in the Silent Unity prayer room answer each telephone call with words of assurance and comfort. In a quiet, confident voice each worker encourages the caller to unburden his or her problem. Words of inspiring advice, a verse of scripture, an affirmation, a prompt prayer—whatever the need, an experienced worker senses the situation and prayerfully replies. At the same time a careful notation is made of the name and address of the caller, with pertinent details regarding the call. This notation is then passed on to another server, who retires to a silent room for prayer. Each worker, of course, has been trained for many years and has dedicated himself or herself to this work of healing.

The calls are of all kinds, expressing every human need. A wife asks prayers for her husband, injured in an automobile accident. Another caller requests aid for a mother in childbirth. Still another requests prayers for someone in a coma. Moment after moment the calls flow in . . .

A few days later a letter will arrive at the caller's home from Silent Unity with the assurance that workers are persisting in prayer for the one in need. Eighty or ninety thousand calls a month mean the same number of letters in reply; whatever the number, letters go out promptly.

It is no wonder that for thousands of people the bright thought of this lighted window is a source of joy and inspiration. For them the light is certain proof in an uncertain world that men and women are at work on this day and in this hour to bring the kingdom of heaven to earth. A visitor who has seen this light shining at night when all others in the village are extinguished says, "Whenever I wake at night and feel the anxieties of life crowding into my thoughts, I remember this light and I am at peace."

Another who has never visited Unity Village but has seen a picture of the lighted window says, "Somehow that picture remains with me all the time. Once I telephoned in the middle of the night for help and a voice answered, promising to pray for my son. For me the light means that somebody cares, somebody is praying."

Had Silent Unity and its prayers been the only achievement of Charles and Myrtle Fillmore, this would be much. There is, however, a great deal more. Millions of pieces of Unity literature go out to the world every month. Perhaps the most cherished of all is *Daily Word*, a pocket-size monthly booklet with prayers and affirmations for each day of the month. *Daily Word* is printed in nine languages and has a circulation of a million copies. It is cherished in the poorest as well as the richest homes in many lands. It can be found in the pockets of the pilots of planes and the pockets of their passengers. Travelers carry it on ships, trains, subways, and buses. Business people have *Daily Word* in their desks; factory workers carry it in their lunch-boxes.

Unity Village covers fourteen hundred acres, or more than two square miles. At the entrance there is a commanding tower one hundred and sixty-five feet high, the highest structure for miles around. Beyond Unity Tower is an open quadrangle between buildings which show the influence of Italian Renaissance architecture. Ash trees line both sides of a long central pool. The administration office, the Silent Unity building, the library, the numerous offices and meeting rooms, the chapel, the cafeteria, the printing plant, the visitors' cottages and motels, the gardens and grounds—all constitute a plant so large that the maintenance force alone numbers eighty workers.

Any one of the Unity enterprises would be a satisfactory life proj-ect, but Charles and Myrtle Fillmore conceived and established all of them through persistence, devotion, faith, and hard work.

Courage in the face of obstacles marks a true pioneer. Because Charles Fillmore had courage and competence his pioneering work proved successful in the end. But that end was not achieved without trials that tested him in every nerve and sinew. Pain and tribulation were his in the beginning, but he developed the staying power to overcome many obstacles in his own life and in the world.

Charles was in his mid-thirties when a serious crisis in his life turned him to the unremitting search for God. At that time Myrtle Fillmore was an invalid who had sought healing from tuberculosis for many years in vain. Charles was a real-estate agent in Kansas City whose business was beginning to fail because of a depression which swept through the Middle West.

When Myrtle Fillmore was in the depths of despair, she turned to New Thought. Her healing and regeneration ultimately impressed Charles, though at first he merely showed a polite interest in her studies. His interest quickened when Myrtle's transformation from chronic invalidism to glowing health also endowed her with the ability to heal others through prayer.

Here was a religion with a practical quality that appealed to Charles Fillmore. He himself had been suffering for over twenty years from lameness, wearing an iron brace to support a right leg which was some three inches shorter than the left. As a boy of ten he had dislocated his hip in a skating accident. The hip and upper thigh of his right leg became infected, and during the ensuing illness the hip joint became fixed. When Charles recovered his right leg was shriveled. The illness had left the right side of his body weak, with hearing and seeing affected in his right ear and eye.

In these circumstances, pilloried by pain and economic stringency, Charles Fillmore sought God. Later he was to emphasize the fundamental nature of this search in many ways, on many occasions. Nothing is more certain than this: Charles studied New Thought, Christian Science, Theosophy, Oriental philosophies, world religions, the metaphysical teachings of many schools, but his single-minded purpose was not to find a system, but to find God.

In this exigency of his life Charles dedicated himself to the study of spiritual Truth and its working principles. He embraced the whole scope of world religions. He studied the great religions of East and West, the mystical philosophies of every era, countless commentaries on the Bible, and the pioneering ideas of New Thought.

Not content with study, Charles spent long hours in meditation and prayer. In time his pain departed, his leg condition improved, and he was ultimately healed.

Throughout his life of ninety-four years he brought a remarkable synthesis to the world of modern metaphysics, blending spiritual healing with a vital and practical religion. It is impossible to overemphasize the fact that Charles Fillmore began his studies some ten or fifteen years before the dawn of the twentieth century, for in making the whole realm of religion his field of knowledge he showed great originality and courage. There were only a few rare thinkers in the world at that time who sought such a comprehensive goal. Even in the 1970s such universality and breadth of knowledge in a teacher is rarely found.

Charles Fillmore's place in American history as an original thinker has yet to be assessed. He embraced ideas of extraordinary scope, including the religious and mystical ideas of the Orient and the Occident, as well as the ideas of the new metaphysics flourishing at the time. Indeed, he went beyond the usual scope of these studies to embrace the scientific discoveries of his day.

Encompassing all the world religions and philosophies in his search, Charles Fillmore finally came to the conclusion that Jesus taught spiritual truths of eternal importance. During his period of study he passed through a severe crisis which he overcame through the Master's teachings. In the overcoming Charles came to know Jesus as the great reality of his own personal life. And so two thousand years after the Master Christian walked the hills of Galilee Charles Fillmore taught as if he were one of the original apostles—John or Andrew or Peter—with direct knowledge of the Master.

And now for the story.

1 The First Seven Years

When Henry Fillmore, an Indian trader, came to the vast Northwest Territory in 1854, he built his cabin near St. Cloud, a hamlet on the banks of the Mississippi. Here Henry saw signs of promising growth, for St. Cloud was the terminus where the Hudson's Bay Company unloaded furs from the great northern wilderness.

The territory was a huge primeval forest. Glaciers of the ice age had scoured the countryside into low hillocks, pocketed with occasional marshes and flowing streams. The rolling hills were covered with colossal pines, white birches, poplars, maples, and oaks.

The Chippewas and the Sioux had been moved into this region by the United States government. Here they hunted and trapped. Henry Fillmore, their trader, had a new cabin by a ford over the Sauk River near its junction with the Mississippi.

At the St. Cloud landing the Mississippi River was about two hundred yards wide. The first squatter had taken possession a year before Henry Fillmore arrived, and had sold his claim to John L. Wilson, a pioneer from Maine.

The name St. Cloud offers that unexpected proof of European culture sometimes found in faraway places throughout the United States. According to the tradition, Wilson was in his cabin reading the life of Napoleon when two French traders knocked at his door.

At that moment Wilson had just come to the point in his book where Napoleon had left Paris to relax at St. Cloud.

"Where are we?" asked the traders when Wilson opened the door.

"St. Cloud!" answered Wilson. And so a settlement in the Northwest Territory was named for Napoleon's favorite palace on the outskirts of Paris.

Shortly after Henry Fillmore came to St. Cloud he married Mary Georgiana Stone. Mary was eighteen years old, the daughter of a millwright who had left Nova Scotia for the far Northwest. The Stone family was of Welsh and English ancestry, and Mary had been reared in the hardworking tradition of her people.

There were no roads in those days, only forest trails leading from one inland settlement to another. Travel was usually by river. The nearest town of any size was St. Anthony, soon to be renamed Minneapolis. It was downriver about 60 miles and was only a sizable village. In all that great Northwest Territory of about 80,000 square miles there were only about 7,000 pioneers of European extraction. Population was flowing in, however, for in 1851, three years before Henry Fillmore arrived in St. Cloud, the Sioux had given up their rights to millions of acres of land west of the Mississippi.

At that time Henry was the only member of his family who had penetrated so far West. Born in Buffalo, he had attended the common schools there, leaving in early manhood for Minnesota.

Millard Fillmore, the thirteenth president of the United States, belonged to another branch of the Fillmore family who were second cousins. When Henry came to St. Cloud, Millard Fillmore had been out of presidential office only a year. A generation earlier one of Henry's uncles, Glezen Fillmore, had been the first ordained Methodist Episcopal minister in New York State and had established the first Methodist Episcopal Church in Buffalo, New York.

As for other ancestors, a certain John Fillmore had been kidnaped by pirates off the coast of England. Many months later he and a companion were able to seize the ship after an orgy in which the pirates drank themselves into a stupor. The two men tied up the pirates and sailed into Boston Harbor, where they sought asylum. The pirates were executed, and the court presented John Fillmore with the captain's sword and cane.

Family traditions, however, were of small importance on the frontier. What Henry Fillmore, the Indian trader, was in himself—that was the important thing. And what Mary Georgiana Fillmore was in herself—that too was of prime importance.

When the summer dawn was flushing the Minnesota sky at 4:00 A.M. on August 22, 1854, Charles Sherlock Fillmore was born.

In preparation for the coming winter Henry Fillmore piled huge stacks of wood outside his cabin door, for a blazing fire was always needed in the fireplace to keep the cabin warm in the 40-degree-below-zero winter temperature. When he grew to manhood Charles would often say with a chuckle, "That fireplace devoured wood like a demon! Every winter my brother Norton and I were kept busy all day feeding that monster."

Charles was about two years old when a band of painted Indians rushed up to the cabin one day and tore him from his mother. The leader, a Sioux medicine man in full headdress and regalia, leaped on his horse with Charles and rode off accompanied by the band.

At sundown, before Henry Fillmore returned home, the Indian warriors brought Charles back to his mother. Charles was too young to remember what the Sioux did with him, but in later life he would say to his friends, "I have always had a feeling that they performed some kind of ceremony with me."

Because of her distress when Charles was kidnaped, Mary Fillmore was never inclined to dwell on it in later years—indeed the family could garner none of the real details. Mary was pregnant at the time. A few months later, when Charles was two years old, his brother Norton was born.

As Charles grew older, he spent much time wandering about the tepees pitched near his father's cabin. What an exciting time young Charles had in those Indian camps! At the age of ninety-four Charles wrote an affirmation which began, "I fairly sizzle with energy." When he was six years old a sizzling young Charles dashed through those camps and played with the Indian boys. There was excitement in the air at that time, an electricity of promise. The Northwest Territory was growing rapidly in population. Minnesota had been granted statehood in 1858, and traders, pioneers, and adventurers were pouring into the land.

So Charles mingled with Indians, hunters, trappers, travelers, and men of all types. He began to develop those outgoing, friendly qualities which made him the universal man of later years.

When Charles was seven his father moved away from their home and built a solitary hut for himself in the forest some ten miles north of the family cabin. Henry Fillmore, it seemed, was a "solitary," one of those migrants who came to the West to seek a place removed from the haunts of their fellowmen, and not merely to find a new and promising environment. After the glamor of a new experience had passed, such men often withdrew from society. They liked loneliness and regarded a solitary life as their prerogative. Usually the society in which they moved accepted their way of life without censure.

Mary Georgiana Fillmore was then twenty-five years old, and she supported her little family with courage and resourcefulness. The difficulty was not so much in finding food as in providing the boys with those necessities which make possible a degree of culture and convenience.

Before her marriage Mary had shown ability as a dressmaker. St. Cloud was growing into a sizable village, and she was able to earn some money designing and sewing dresses.

Food was not a major problem. Wild animals were plentiful, and Henry Fillmore supplied the family with a certain amount of game. Game could also be obtained from hunters and trappers. Charles and Norton gathered food from the countryside. Like the Indians, they would gather wild rice in a canoe, bending the rice blades over the edge and beating the grain off into sacks. They became competent fishermen. They gathered wild berries, cranberries, and other fruit in season. Potatoes and beans were family staples. Often the stew was thin. Mary Fillmore could make a few bones and some beans go a long way, and she fed her children regularly.

There is a school of thought which emphasizes the importance of the first seven years of a child's life. Some categorical statements are made regarding the supreme effects of these early years; however that may be, Charles had developed self-reliance and courage by the time he was seven.

In spite of her stringent circumstances Mary Fillmore saw to it that Charles attended the log-cabin school in their district. Perhaps more than any other event this single circumstance casts light on Mary's character. It would have been easy to keep Charles home, to declare that she needed all the help her seven-year-old son could give her; to let self-pity take over. But Mary saw to it that Charles went to school. It was a one-room school, with one schoolmaster. The term lasted for only three months during the middle period of winter.

The opportunity to attend church was rare, so Charles had little formal religious training. Mary Fillmore, however, was a deeply religious woman, an Episcopalian who knew the Litanies of her church by heart. It was the sterling patience of his mother that met Charles' need—a patience which he acquired by a kind of soul-absorption.

2 The Valley of the Shadow

As we have seen, when Charles was about ten years old he fell in a skating accident which proved fraught with dire results. The fall injured his hip. He may have dislocated the bone in its socket, he may have torn the ligaments, or he may have damaged the cartilage. No one knows, for in those days, without X rays, such conditions were hard to diagnose.

His damaged hip failed to heal, and Charles grew worse month by month. His mother desperately sought all the medical aid she could find. One doctor thought that the ailment was rheumatic and his treatment failed. Other doctors came and went. Each doctor had his own diagnosis and his own treatment, all in vain. Charles' pain was constant, and he developed complications.

In Charles' young frame the battle was joined between the forces of life and death. The same principle was involved in the battle which Job of old had fought for his own survival. The ordeal of the young boy and the struggle of the mature man had this in common: each was a naked battle for life.

Where there is a struggle for survival there is a profound human principle at stake, and this is why the struggle of Job has had such a vital meaning for those who seek soul values. History tells us of famous men who have struggled with pain and disease and have won their fight, gaining qualities in their ordeal that have enabled them to rise to heights of attainment. St. Ignatius of Loyola among the saints, for instance, and Franklin Delano Roosevelt among world leaders faced death and won the battle, meeting life henceforth with a courage that nothing could daunt. Young Charles with his wasted frame was engaged in the same struggle.

For two years after his fall he fought the disease encroaching on his life. At times the boy wept silent tears of agony.

With his mother's help he made a pair of crutches, and when he could manage it, he hopped around the cabin to help her. At other times he remained in bed because of discomfort and weakness. He clung to a thread of life in spite of all, and though there were days when he could have gone under merely by letting go, somehow he held on.

A pernicious characteristic of the disease was its ebb and flow. There were times when Charles would think he had conquered the disease, only to have it return with greater violence.

Gradually, however, the insidious, weakening effect of the infection began to wane. There came a day when Charles' strength began to increase, and he could walk with less pain. His right leg had stopped growing, but he was alive! He was now a boy of twelve, and the spirit of life within him had won. He had walked through the valley of the shadow of death. His new steps were feeble, and he walked with the aid of crutches. But he was walking into life. He had quaffed his cup of pain and the gall had given way to sweetness. Life was sweet.

3 Study and Work

Describing his condition many years later, Charles said, "I was bled, leached, cupped, lanced, seasoned, blistered, and roweled. Six running sores were artificially produced on my leg to draw out the diseased condition that was presumed to be within." At another time he added, "It's a miracle to me how I ever got away from those doctors with the little bundle of bones and sinews that I found in my possession after they had finished their experiments."

In maturity Charles was slender and wiry in build, so that in his convalescence as a boy of twelve he must have been a gaunt figure.

Very seldom, however, could Charles be persuaded to speak of those days. When he did it was always in a light vein. One of his close friends says, "He had a bright smile, and even when he spoke of his pain he would bring in a little humor, and add some whimsical touch."

Near the end of Charles' illness his younger brother Norton ran away from home, never to return. After Norton left, Charles grew closer to his mother, helping her in every way. Now Mary and her twelve-year-old son were alone. Charles had become the man of the family.

Throughout this period of suffering a deep bond had been established between Charles and his mother. Day after day Mary Georgiana Fillmore's stability and compassion had helped him physically, and she imparted to him her ingrained courage and serenity.

"Now you must go back to school," said Mary, and Charles returned to St. Cloud's one-room school on his crutches.

After two years, however, Charles had to leave school and go to work in order to help his mother. Fortunately, there were jobs in St. Cloud, now an expanding village. People had begun to flow into town when it was linked with Minneapolis by rail in 1866, and in 1868, about the time Charles went to work, it had a population of some three thousand people.

His first job was with a printer. A printer's devil in those days did everything from sweeping the floor to cleaning type and running the hand press. It is said that the smell of printing ink with its pungent odor can never be forgotten, and Providence seems to have been on Charles' side when he found his first job in the printing trade. About twenty years later when a turning point came in his life he returned to the printing business and produced a magazine, *Modern Thought*.

Charles' next job was in a grocery store, and after that he worked in a bank.

In St. Cloud Charles found a companion of his own age, Edgar Taylor. The boys spent much time together. Happily, Edgar's mother, Caroline Taylor, took a liking to Charles and within a short time she became his benefactor. Mrs. Taylor, who had attended Oberlin College, was tutoring her son Edgar. As the son of an army officer he was destined for the army and his education was important. Caroline Taylor's tutoring was as thorough as she could make it, and because she found Charles compatible she tutored him with her son.

Mrs. Taylor introduced Charles to the classics as well as to the great writers of the day. Charles plunged into Shakespeare, learning to love drama and poetry—Tennyson, Shelley, the Brownings. For him it was the discovery of a new world of infinite scope, and he gloried in it. Charles took James Russell Lowell and Ralph Waldo Emerson into his young heart. Later he named his first son Lowell, his second son Waldo.

Mrs. Taylor taught Charles the rules of grammar, gave him writing assignments, pointed out his errors, awoke in him an appreciation of language. Charles had to make his meanings clear, to reduce difficult ideas to simple sentences.

This early discipline taught Charles a simplicity from which he never departed. In mature life, when his writings became popular, Charles always took great pains to express complex ideas in simple, practical language. Friends who noted his style of speaking have told me that sometimes when he was lecturing he would stop at the beginning of a sentence and remain silent, collecting his thoughts in order to express them in simple language.

Another feature of Caroline Taylor's tutelage was to assume importance in later years. She introduced Charles to advanced ideas which were raising eyebrows in New England. Bronson Alcott was questioning old theological beliefs. Ralph Waldo Emerson had retired from his pastorate because he could not agree with some of the theological ideas he was expected to promulgate from the pulpit. In New England transcendentalism was coming to birth; agnosticism was gaining ground. Robert Ingersoll was delivering lectures deemed heretical by churchgoers. Caroline Taylor did not conceal such original ideas from her young pupil, so Charles Fillmore learned to ask searching questions about orthodox theology when he was still in his teens.

It is hardly possible to overestimate the importance of this tutoring period for Charles. Who can gauge the influence of a good tutor on a receptive pupil?

As Charles grew to manhood he began to view St. Cloud with new eyes. His knowledge of books and other cultures was wider than the views of other young men in town, thanks to his tutor. He had been printer's devil, had worked in a grocery and a bank, but something within him said that his destiny was not in St. Cloud. His mind turned toward the outside world and he talked the situation over with his mother.

Mary Georgiana Fillmore knew her son, and she agreed that the time had come for him to leave. When Charles said, "I will send for you, Mother, as soon as I can," she smiled and said, "Do what you must do, my son."

Towns were going up overnight in the Far West, railroads were opening up new lands, gold and silver mines were being discovered. So Charles decided to go West. He had a cousin in the town of Caddo near the Texas border in Indian Territory. As he was approaching his twentieth year, in the spring of 1874, Charles took the train out of St. Cloud for the fifteen-hundred-mile trip to Caddo. Whether his lameness would hinder him was left to be seen, but Charles was sure of one thing: It would not be a handicap so far as he was concerned.

4 "There's Your Wife, Charles"

In spite of his shortened leg, fixed in its hip socket, Charles was a spry young man. There were times when he was in pain, but he never let anyone know. Of medium height, slender, with shining blue eyes, he moved as if unconscious of his limp. He knew that if he was to make his way in the West he would have to rise above his physical handicap and prove himself in his own way.

Caddo turned out to be a wild frontier town—it was one of the wildest—with no amenities, and Charles soon moved on twenty miles south to Denison, Texas. Here the chief clerk of the freight office of the Missouri, Kansas and Texas Railroad took a liking to Charles and gave him a job. Denison was the railroad terminus, with freight cars ever on the move in and out of the yards.

Charles spent much time in the freight yards checking bills of lading, identifying the cars, totaling packages and barrels and bags, learning the freight business. It was a job demanding alertness and accuracy, and Charles became a competent checker. In addition, he went beyond mere detail. He was interested in the way the freight was controlled, and he was often in the office of the chief clerk, helping him with his duties and discovering how the yard was run.

Later when Charles spoke of these days he would remark, "Sometimes my friends laughed at me! They joked about my willingness to work late. 'Come on, Charles,' they would say, 'a day's work is enough!' In fact a few of them accused me of playing up to the boss."

"And what did you say?" a friend once asked Charles.

"I kept on with what I was doing," Charles replied.

When the chief clerk became ill, Charles was the only one who knew how to do his job. Later, when the chief did not return to the office, Charles was appointed in his place.

Now that Charles was settled, he sent for his mother. In Denison Mary Fillmore did more than housekeeping, for she was able to help Charles with her earnings as a dressmaker.

Economic sufficiency enabled Charles to pursue his reading interests—poetry, literature, and philosophy. He joined the social circles of young adults in Denison with similar tastes. They met regularly to discuss literature, to read poetry, and also to recite verses of their own.

Charles enjoyed these meetings. "Would you believe it?" he was to declare later. "They listened while I recited James Russell Lowell and Edgar Allen Poe!"

One of these literary evenings in 1876 proved to be a unique event in Charles' life. A gracious, auburn-haired young woman recited a poem for the group, and as Charles listened admiringly, a voice within him said, *"There's your wife, Charles."*

The young woman with the auburn hair was Myrtle Page, a teacher in a private school in Denison. She had been christened Mary Caroline, but she preferred her father's pet name "Myrtilee," and always used the name Myrtle.

Myrtle Page was born in Pagetown, Ohio, on August 6, 1845. She was the youngest of the nine children of Marcus and Lucy Page. As the name of her birthplace indicates, her family had been early settlers in the town. They were members of the Methodist Episcopal Church, in which Myrtle was raised.

Myrtle's education was advanced for girls of her time, for she had taken the "Literary Course for Ladies" at Oberlin College. Upon leaving Oberlin she went to live for a time with her brother David Page in Clinton, Missouri. Later she moved to Denison.

Myrtle Page and Charles Fillmore soon discovered that they liked the same books, the same verses of poetry, the same new ideas appearing on the literary horizon of the time. They shared an interest in the latest scientific discoveries and theories. Together they delighted in picnicking and searching for fossils.

Those picnics were bright hours for Charles. He treasured the memory of the voice that had told him, *"There's your wife, Charles."* He began seriously to consider his economic status and the possibility of leaving the freight office to seek a wider career. He would await the right opportunity.

A change in Myrtle's affairs came in 1878 when her teaching job ended. She decided to return to Clinton, Missouri, where she could resume teaching. The parting was physical, not mental, and a stream of letters flowed between Charles and Myrtle.

Many of these letters, lengthy by our modern standards, were vibrant with their reactions to life and events and ideas.

These two bared their inner lives and thoughts to each other in many delicate ways. In answer to one of Charles' letters, for instance, Myrtle revealed this inmost self in full confidence: "Now, I seldom dare confess to this foolish (?) other life I keep within myself, but I couldn't live without it. And when I try to choke it out, I am the most miserable creature on earth."*

One day in 1879 an executive of the railroad came through Denison on an inspection trip. During his visit he made false charges against one of the workers. The man was Charles' friend and Charles came to his aid. The executive was outraged, but Charles would not yield. Firmly he insisted that the man was not at˙fault. A tense argument ensued, and Charles lost his job.

Charles was free at last to move on to a new venture. He was

*James Dillet Freeman, *The Household of Faith*.

intrigued with Colorado, which had achieved statehood in 1876—the centennial year of the Declaration of Independence. Adopting the title, "The Centennial State," Colorado was welcoming newcomers. The discovery of gold had brought a flood of new arrivals into the state, and the recent discovery of silver produced a still greater influx. There were fabulous stories of fortunes made in a day, so Charles set out for Colorado.

In that raw territory a man took whatever job he could find. A Wild-West novelist would have been hard put to conceive of the job that Charles Fillmore found for himself. He hired on as a mule-team driver.

Charles' limp could not be hidden, for he wore an iron brace to aid his short leg. The owner of the freight line must have seen something in Charles Fillmore superior to his physical disability. A mule-team driver must have endurance and stamina; the wiry frame of Charles must have revealed a certain quality of will superior to heavy muscularity.

The mountain roads had not been laid out by government road surveyors, but had started as Indian trails. They were widened for horses and widened again for mule teams when a mine was started. Sharp turns with a mountain on one side and a gorge on the other made the descent of a loaded team dangerous. At times even the best drivers lost control of the mules on a steep downgrade. Then the driver, with explosive *whoa's* and brakes clamped tight, would drop his reins and jump for his life.

On one occasion Charles had to do this, and whenever he related the story he would say in the bland, casual voice of a good story-teller, "Once my mules, wagon and all, went off the edge of a precipice and I had to fling myself from the wagon to save my skin."

During long freight hauls Charles slept under the wagon. The nights were windy and cold, so he hung a tarpaulin over the sides of the wagon to make a shelter. He ate jerky, beans, and bread, and kept healthy. His leg caused him pain, but he never told anyone.

The town of Gunnison had just been plotted in 1879 when Charles began to bring in his freight loads. Within a few months he gave up his mule-team job and went to Leadville, Colorado, to take a course in metallurgy so that he could become a mining assayer. While he accomplished this aim Gunnison became a boomtown. Buildings went up overnight. New mines brought an influx of prospectors and mine workers and soon Gunnison showed signs of becoming a stable town.

Charles saw great opportunities in the real-estate business and he became a real-estate operator. All the time, of course, he kept writing Myrtle, while she in turn kept up their correspondence in a lively, sympathetic vein. Within two years Charles was well established in his business, and at last he was able to make the trip to Clinton, Missouri, to bring Myrtle home as his wife.

On March 29, 1881, Charles Fillmore and Myrtle Page were married in the little Methodist church in Clinton. They pronounced their vows, and as Charles turned to Myrtle, the voice he had heard five years earlier again echoed in his ears: *"There's your wife, Charles."*

5 Myrtle Fillmore's Healing

Myrtle Fillmore enjoyed the trip across the Continental Divide, which she called "The Delectable Mountains." First Myrtle and Charles traveled by rail, then after a two-day rest at the end of the railroad line they transferred to a stagecoach. The mountain passes were filled with snow, and the couple changed again—this time to a huge horse-drawn sleigh in order to cross the divide. Parts of this trip were dangerous because the roads were slippery and treacherous. When they finally arrived in Gunnison a week passed before the next coach was able to cross the mountains.

About a year after Charles and Myrtle were married, economic conditions in Gunnison changed. The promising real-estate market unexpectedly collapsed. Several mines failed, the price of land dropped, and people began to leave town. Charles, the real-estate operator, had land to sell but suddenly there were no buyers.

Pueblo, Colorado, however, was booming. Steel works had begun operation, and since ore was plentiful in the region the town was becoming an industrial center. Pueblo was a hundred and fifty miles away, on the other side of the Continental Divide, so Charles and Myrtle crossed the mountains again. He arrived in Pueblo with only ten cents in his pocket.

First Charles found lodgings for himself and Myrtle. Next he went to a grocery store and ordered goods to be delivered to his new lodgings. "Please deliver them C.O.D.," said Charles. Then he walked out into the streets of Pueblo and took a deep breath to see what he could find.

There in the streets of Pueblo Charles found a friend from whom he borrowed ten dollars.

Back to the grocer went Charles. "Ah, there you are!" exclaimed the grocer. "My boy went to deliver the groceries, but your wife had no money so he brought them back."

Charles gazed at the grocer, conveying perfect astonishment.

"Well . . .," began the grocer, but said no more as Charles casually reached into his pocket, paying for the groceries as if the money were a mere trifle.

The grocer took the money, and while he was making change Charles looked around the store with much interest.

"I see that you have some space over there," he remarked. "I am interested in renting some space. You see, I am in the real-estate business and I want to set up an office in town."

"Real-estate business?" echoed the owner of the store. "Why, that's wonderful!" One thing led to another, and by the time Charles left he had rented the space on credit.

Then Charles hired a wagon. Decorating it with bright yellow cloth, he painted his name in large red letters on the cloth banners and announced the opening of his new real-estate office.

Pueblo smiled and took Charles Fillmore to its heart. Within a short time his business was flourishing.

A year later, in 1882, the couple's first child was born—Lowell Page Fillmore. Two years later came a second son—Waldo Rickert Fillmore.

Then suddenly the scene in Pueblo changed. Several gold and silver mines in the area shut down because they had been worked to the limit. Though there was a steel plant in town, its laborers were immigrants who worked in the mills at low wages. They had arrived in Pueblo with all their worldly goods wrapped in small bundles, and they were too poor to live in anything but shacks. Once again history repeated itself and Charles lost his business.

As before, Charles acted without delay. He salvaged what he could and together with his small family left Pueblo as promptly as he had left Gunnison.

They stopped for a few weeks during the summer in Omaha, Nebraska, but in the winter of 1884 moved on to Kansas City, Missouri. Here Charles felt he could establish a real-estate business free from the boom-and-bust perils of pioneer towns.

The real-estate business in Kansas City was flourishing. The city was a port of entry for goods from northern and western states, and its central location in the vast prairie region made it one of the fastest-growing cities in the Middle West.

When Charles arrived in 1884, Kansas City had doubled its population in the past ten years, and it continued to expand at the same rate. The excitement of growth was in the air. Real-estate values were soaring. Office buildings, lots, and choice acreages were being sold and resold in a few days at a substantial profit. Farms on the outskirts of the expanding city were selling at downtown prices. And the cost of downtown city parcels soared higher everyday.

Within a short time Charles' experience in real estate made him a prosperous operator. He began to take part in the development of the city. Histories of Kansas City at this time speak of Fillmore and Company. Charles acquired land in the northeast section of the city where he laid out a subdivision, Gladstone Heights. Streets in Kansas City still bear the names Charles gave them, as Myrtle Avenue, named in honor of his wife, and Norton Avenue, named for his brother.

His prosperity assured, Charles had prospects of becoming wealthy. He dressed in a simple quiet style, eschewing some of the cavalier modes. The dandies of the day wore high collars, handle-bar mustaches, and hair curled or brushed downward to cover their foreheads. Charles wore medium collars, a well-trimmed mustache, and a finely trimmed beard. His hair was combed back, a style which befitted his broad full forehead. He was slim and wiry, and his walk was agile despite his limp.

But all was not well with the Fillmores physically. Besides the discomfort of the iron brace which Charles wore for his short leg, the sight in his right eye began to fail. And Myrtle, who had not been well for some years, was becoming worse. She had never been robust; her condition had been repeatedly diagnosed as incipient tuberculosis. Now malaria was sapping her energies. Myrtle began to despair.

Grandma Fillmore came to Kansas City and took charge of the domestic duties, cooking for the family and helping Myrtle with Lowell and Rickert.

With the hope of improving Myrtle's health, Charles decided to take a summer trip to Colorado. In Silverton there was a mine in which he had retained partnership, and Charles took his wife and Lowell with him to the mountains. Grandma Fillmore remained at home to care for Rickert.

The small family lived in a tent high up in the mountains, packing in what they needed on burros. The mine failed to show further promise, and Charles spent some time prospecting. In the fall Myrtle's health was somewhat improved, so the family returned to Kansas City.

Charles found that a financial depression had begun to settle over the Middle West and that the city had lost its economic momentum. Real-estate prices were falling; there were no purchasers for available land; both the city and the state were in the throes of a painful economic adjustment. Droughts had hurt the farmers for several years in succession. Grain prices had fallen to the point where it was unprofitable for a farmer to raise wheat or corn.

Once again Charles began to lose his capital and to see economic difficulties ahead.

Perhaps the most agonizing crises that occur in family life come about when financial stringency coincides with illness. Such a crisis now faced the Fillmores.

Myrtle's health had declined after her return to Kansas City. What had been deemed incipient tuberculosis became an active condition. The malaria which she had contracted as a young woman recurred with violence. Myrtle had tried many doctors, many medicines, and now they could help her no more. Darkness enveloped her.

Charles thought of returning to Colorado, where the climate might be better for Myrtle. He had many friends in the state and felt that it should not be difficult for him to earn a living there.

Then a vivid dream caused him to change his mind about moving from Kansas City.

"I had a strange dream," Charles declared. "An unseen voice said, 'Follow me.' I was led up and down the hilly streets of Kansas City and my attention was called to localities I was familiar with. The Presence stopped and said: 'You will remember having had a dream some years ago in which you were shown this city and told you had a work to do here. Now you are being reminded of that dream and also informed that the invisible power that has located you will continue to be with you and aid you in the appointed work.' When I awoke, I remembered that I had such a dream and had forgotten it."

There is an age-old tradition in both the East and the West that when a prophetic dream is repeated the prophecy is of great consequence. Charles accepted the importance of his second dream and decided to remain in Kansas City.

Myrtle had been given only six months to live. Just when there seemed no way to turn, a friend said to her, "Why not try New Thought? Dr. Weeks is speaking in town. I have heard him and I think you may get some help from him."

So Myrtle and Charles attended the lecture of Dr. E. B. Weeks one spring evening in 1886, and Myrtle heard a message which illumined her darkness. One bright sentence uplifted her, and when she left the hall she was walking on air into a new life, repeating the words: "I am a child of God and therefore I do not inherit sickness."

6 Myrtle Fillmore's Rebirth

Only those who have been lost in the night of fear can know the joy that leaps within the heart when a light shines through the gloom. The heart's prayer is answered—to walk toward the light is to walk toward warmth and safety. From the moment she caught its first gleam in the darkness of disease and despair, Myrtle Fillmore walked unhesitatingly toward the light.

"I am a child of God and therefore I do not inherit sickness"—that was her constant refrain. Day and night she sang the words until at last they brought her freedom. Though her healing took time, she never wavered.

Charles had paid attention to the lecture, but he had listened with the mind of a businessman. The difficulty through which he was passing was a problem of finance, not a matter of life or death. For Myrtle the question was life or death.

Describing her condition at that time, she often said, "I was an emaciated woman, upon whom relatives and doctors had placed the stamp of tuberculosis."

Myrtle devoted all her energies to the investigation of the metaphysical principles taught by Dr. Weeks. She devoured all the available literature. Hourly and daily she affirmed that she was a child of God. Her complete healing took about a year, but in the end she became the embodiment of health.

Not only was Myrtle's transformation physical, it was also mental and spiritual. She ensouled the truths which she recognized, and finally expressed them so fully that she gained the ability to heal.

Then a still more fundamental change in her life began. As her neighbors came to Wabash Avenue to hear about her transformation, Myrtle's explanations became healing affirmations and prayers. Soon her prayers began to heal all kinds of disease.

An Irishman named Caskey who lived opposite the Fillmores was crippled and was forced to use crutches. At first he did not fully comprehend what Myrtle said about the possibility of his healing, though they prayed together several times. To Myrtle's admonition that he put down his crutches and walk, Mr. Caskey kept on making doubtful replies. But at last one day he grasped the significance of her command when she told him to lay aside his crutches. Casting them aside, he walked across the room and was made whole.

Many years later Mr. Caskey recognized Lowell Fillmore walking down a street in Kansas City. Driving up beside him in a wagon, Caskey stopped and jumped down to speak to him. "Aren't you Lowell Fillmore?" he inquired. "I am Mr. Caskey, the man whom your mother prayed with and healed."

The Fillmores' laundress had asthma, and when Myrtle told her how to pray and promised to help her through prayer, she was soon healed.

One day a salesman came to Myrtle's door selling picture frames and molding. He was invited into the house and was displaying his frames when young Lowell pressed forward to see the display.

"I have a little boy like yours and he will never see again," the salesman remarked.

"Do not say that!" Myrtle replied. "Your boy is a child of God. As a child of God it is his right to see."

"But the doctors say he will never be able to see," the salesman declared.

"Have you ever prayed for him?" Myrtle asked. "God heals every disease."

"Would you pray for my son? Would you come to see him?" the salesman asked.

"I shall be glad to come," Myrtle replied.

On her first visit to the salesman's home Myrtle saw cataracts like the white of an egg covering his son's eyes. She was not dismayed, but prayed with the boy. Working with him, Myrtle taught him to repeat that he was the child of God. She made him say again and again that God loved him, and that God's will for him was perfection, including perfect sight.

By her second visit, the boy had improved enough to greet her at the door and let her in. Soon the cataracts vanished and the boy's sight was restored.

Many other healings took place as Myrtle Fillmore prayed with her neighbors and with others who came to her for help. Now they were coming to her from all parts of the city.

Charles Fillmore's benevolent and somewhat casual interest in metaphysics changed to alert inquiry. Myrtle's healing had impressed him, but her ability to heal awoke in him a dawning sense of the practicability of spiritual healing. Whatever it might be called, New Thought, or Christian Science, or Metaphysics, the pragmatic nature of this new movement stirred him.

Could he, Charles Fillmore, be healed of his apparently incurable condition?

So Charles began his own studies, analyzing the new metaphysical teachings every step of the way. If there was a discovery to be made he would make it in his own way, under his own steam.

7 Charles Fillmore's Search

When Charles Fillmore began to examine the whole field of modern Metaphysics he did not stop there, but enlarged his study to include all the religions of the world. He investigated Buddhism and Hinduism. Then he went on to include such occult studies as Theosophy and Rosicrucianism, a task by no means easy since occult books at that time were few, immature in presentation, and obfuscated in style.

Today it is difficult for us to grasp the magnitude of Charles' task. Only a few years ago Arnold J. Toynbee, writing about a new book, *The Religious Experience of Mankind* by Ninian Smart, declared that its accurate and copious information could not have been compiled, "say, sixty years ago."* To many readers this was a startling bit of information. Toynbee's sixty years ago would be 1909, whereas Charles began his search in the 1880s.

Those who have not made such an investigation can scarcely realize its arduous nature. A hundred years ago it was a stupendous project. Even now many who make the attempt become baffled or weary and give up the search.

During this period, from about 1886 to 1888, Charles threaded his

*In *The New York Times Book Review*, February 9, 1969.

way through a maze of studies without bias, without prejudice, without preconceived judgments.

Diverse ambiguities in these systems of thought and genetic differences among them did not deter him.

"The muddle was so dense," Charles said later, "that for a time I was inclined to ridicule, yet I couldn't get away from the evidence of a great power back of the flood of contradictory statements."

He was honest about his doubts. Nor was he ever ashamed of them. In later years he would say, "Although I was a chronic invalid and seldom free from pain, the doctrine [New Thought] did not at first appeal to me."

We can appreciate these doubts in the light of Charles' early studies with Mrs. Edgar Taylor, his tutor in St. Cloud. For when Mrs. Taylor had introduced him to the advanced ideas of the day, she had opened a door which led to Robert Ingersoll's agnostic writings as well as to Emerson's essays.

Finally there came a time in his studies when Charles made a decision which has proved as important for Unity students as Luther's great statement, "Here I stand, I can do no else."

Charles said, "In this babel I will go to headquarters. If I am Spirit and this God they talk about so much is Spirit, we can somehow communicate, or the whole thing is a fraud."

In this crucial statement Charles not only expressed the standpoint which he maintained for himself, but also the standpoint which he later taught his students to establish for themselves.

Always he said to them, "What I tell you must also appeal to your own understanding." Always he made it clear that he expected them to "go to headquarters" themselves. He taught them how to go to God, and exerted no authority. Today those who knew him best speak of him as a man whose friendliness and Christlike wisdom drew them into his circle. They speak not of his authority, but of his humor and warmth.

In the midst of these religious studies Charles' economic affairs worsened. Kansas City had stopped expanding. Real-estate sales were practically nonexistent. Missouri and other Midwestern states were still deep in the trough of an economic depression. In the mining industries silver had fallen in price, and gold production had fallen off. A long hard fight to maintain a decent standard of living faced the merchants of the city and the farmers of the Middle West.

So once more, through no fault or lack of vision on his part, Charles was in the middle of "a boom that had gone bust." He had seen the real-estate business in Gunnison collapse. He had seen the real-estate business in the promising town of Pueblo collapse. Here in Kansas City real estate had seemed to be the safest of ventures. The location of the city on the Missouri River, and indeed the growth of the whole of the Middle West, seemed to promise a business with an expanding future. Charles had accumulated $150,000 in the real-estate business and it had all gone in the crash. He was in debt. He had looked forward to growing with Kansas City, but now it had stopped growing.

He could not forget that prophetic dream about his destiny in Kansas City, however, so Charles decided not to move. He was in his mid-thirties, and he had weathered financial storms before.

Myrtle knew their stringent circumstances, but now she had faith in the goodness of God and His infinite care. With Grandma Fillmore's help they would make ends meet. To Grandma Fillmore economy was no new demand. From the leftovers of meals she produced miraculously new dishes; she could do wonders with a handful of rice and beans. Grandma was taking care of Lowell and Rickert more and more these days because Myrtle would soon have another child.

Happily, Myrtle was now well—better than she had ever been in her life. Her metaphysical studies had transformed her into a new woman and her sympathy encouraged Charles.

Charles read far into the night, night after night, sometimes until dawn. At length he began to meditate—not to enter into some trance condition, nor to escape from the world, but to seek expansion of consciousness and competence to handle the affairs of the world. Myrtle's healing had been the result of a divine principle at work, and he must understand and grasp that principle for himself. So Charles prayed continuously and worked for his own deeper understanding and healing.

When he described his methods later, he said, "I sat in the silence every night at a certain hour and tried to get in touch with God. I was there on time every night and tried in all conceivable ways to realize that my mind was in touch with the Supreme Mind."

This statement of Charles, "I was there on time every night," describes him to perfection. He was also frank, for he often added, "At first I did not seem to get any conscious result, but I kept at it month after month, mentally affirming words that others told me would open the way, until it got to be a habit and I rather enjoyed it."

At last a time came when Charles began to feel results. He noticed a change for the better in his physical condition. He said, "My chronic pains ceased. My hip healed and grew stronger."

No one had ever known of his chronic pains. Now that they were gone he could speak of them. Now he had convincing proof of the practical nature of spiritual truth.

But these were not Charles Fillmore's only ailments. In his search for perfection he recognized that he must eliminate all his physical difficulties. Inasmuch as the whole right side of his body was weak, his prayers deepened in intensity and fervor.

Soon hearing began to return to the right ear, and improved vision to the right eye. A few years later he would dispense with the four-inch iron brace for his leg. From hip to knee his flesh had been a kind of glassy adhesion with little sensation, but feeling would return and the flesh and muscle would fill out.

His tangible improvement was the thread which Charles held in his hand and followed until it finally led him out of the maze of old anxieties and doubts. He devoted himself more and more to spiritual research.

"My interest became so pronounced," he declared later, "that I neglected my real-estate business for the furtherance of what my friends denounced as a fanatical delusion."

It is sometimes difficult to say when one phase of a man's life gives way to another, but when Charles began to neglect his business activities for metaphysical studies even though demands upon him in the declining real-estate market were acute, he had emerged from his valley of decision.

He paid no attention to the ridicule of his friends and continued on his way. He was climbing a trail with his eye on the heights, imbued with the certainty that no matter the difficulties he would remain in the valley no longer. There was a Mount of Illumination and he would scale its heights.

The time came at last when Charles began to integrate the essential teachings of many spiritual traditions and to weave them into an inspiring pattern. He began to achieve a synthesis that would bless the world.

Not at once did this synthesis appear, for there was much work to be done. There was still a vast complex of ideas to coordinate. There was an idiom to be worked out, and this would be a consummate task, for Charles wished to achieve simplicity. There was a glossary of terms to be compiled. There were profound ideas to be expressed, difficult definitions to be made clear.

Even so, Charles came to a brave decision: He would publish a magazine!

Perhaps memories of his first job as a printer's devil at the age of fourteen helped him to conceive this project. He knew something of the work involved and what had to be done. There was so much burgeoning within Charles that a magazine seemed the right outlet for his ideas.

He would continue his real-estate business, for that was his livelihood. He would divide his time somehow between real estate and publishing, and he would have to do much of the work himself. The capital would come out of his meager financial earnings in a depressed real-estate market, with no sales coming in. Every penny that he used would be a penny out of the family's slender means. The employees were Myrtle and himself. Happily, Myrtle was in perfect agreement with his idea, but the spadework would have to be his.

There was paper to be bought, so Charles found an economical source of supply. There was typesetting to be done, so he found Mr. Palmer, who could work in his own home setting up fonts of type. Though Mr. Palmer had another job, the fonts were his and could be set on his own time. Then the heavy fonts had to be moved to the printer, and this Charles did himself.

Fonts must be moved with care for a jolt or a spill will disarrange or mix the type, causing whole pages to have to be reset. All this was hard muscular labor for one of Charles' build. But the man who had driven a mule team was equal to the task.

This spadework was only the physical part of the task. The editorial policy had to be set and maintained by Charles; the articles had to be of his choosing, or Myrtle's. A good mailing list had to be secured for the first issues. Advertisements had to be solicited, so Charles canvassed and sold them.

What would be the name of the magazine?

"*Modern Thought!*" The name rolled on Charles' tongue, and Myrtle wholeheartedly approved.

Myrtle wrote for the magazine, using the initial "M". Charles wrote the editorial, as he would write other editorials for years to come. The publishing headquarters was Charles' real-estate office in the old Journal Building at Walmuth and Tenth Streets.

With no other help, Charles and Myrtle produced the first issue in April 1889, and *Modern Thought* was born.

8 Unity Is Born

The title page of *Modern Thought* bore a courageous motto: "Devoted to the Spiritualization of Humanity from an Independent Standpoint."

Never did Charles Fillmore waver from this purpose. The motto was in fact the escutcheon of the man. These two basic ideas of the motto were to be his lifework henceforth. First: The "Spiritualization of Humanity"; second: the "Independent Standpoint" of a teacher who would continually "go to headquarters" and encourage all men to do likewise.

Events proved that Charles had truly sensed a spiritual demand of his times. Had *Modern Thought* not supplied a genuine need it would never have survived to this day. No longer called *Modern Thought*, today it is *Unity*, with a history of continuous publication which makes it one of the oldest magazines in the United States.

The magazine was thirteen by nine inches, with sixteen pages divided into three columns. A year's subscription cost one dollar, a single issue one dime. That first issue in April 1889 was a compendium of contemporary Metaphysics, New Thought, Christian Science, occultism, and Theosophy.

And yet it was more than a compendium. There was a lilt in that first editorial, a promise of things to come, a sparkling tonality in the choice of articles, awakening interest like the first chord of a symphony. There could be no doubt that there was a guiding mind—an interesting mind—at work at the editor's desk. The proof of this engaging quality was in the spontaneous response of readers. Something awakened a favorable reaction in them. They wrote letters, sent in partial payments, asked for more issues.

The first issue had noticeable typographical errors. In the second issue Charles apologized for them with a touch of whimsy. The typographical errors continued, however, for there was no professional proofreader. Charles was writer, purchasing agent, advertising manager, salesman, editor, and proofreader all in one. Both Charles and Myrtle worked for several months without any clerical help. They could not afford a stenographer. Soon the letters were too numerous for them to answer, but readers continued to show interest in *Modern Thought*.

Five months after the first issue, in September 1889, Charles moved his publishing offices to larger quarters in the Deardorff Building at Eleventh and Main Streets. Charles then inserted a WANT AD for a young man or woman to set type. He promised "a home and small wages." Perhaps the "small wages" caused no response.

Myrtle's help during the summer was somewhat limited. As the July issue of *Modern Thought* was going through the mails, Royal Fillmore was born on July 5, 1889.

All the money that the Fillmores took in went out as fast as it came. That Christmas in 1889 Myrtle Fillmore faced the bare prospect of having no money to buy presents for her children. A few days before Christmas a neighbor stopped by and insisted on paying Myrtle five dollars for the help and comfort she had received. So Myrtle bought seven-year-old Lowell a tool chest, five-year-old Rick a drum, a sword, and a military hat. A friend sent them a box which arrived on Christmas Eve, and the family celebrated the holiday with joy.

January 1890 marked only ten months of publication, but so many readers were writing in for information, and so many people in

Kansas City were asking for prayer and personal counseling, that Charles and Myrtle were teaching, editing, and practicing spiritual healing through prayer—all at the same time.

That month an event of special importance took place in their lives. Emma Curtis Hopkins visited Kansas City for the first time to lecture and teach. A student of hers, Dr. Weeks, had started the transformation of Myrtle with the message: "I am a child of God and therefore I do not inherit sickness."

Emma Curtis Hopkins, teacher of teachers, was tall and dignified, but when she lectured her warmth and eloquence enfolded her students and inspired them. Not many women could wear the wide-brimmed hats of that day with grace on the lecture platform, but Emma Curtis Hopkins wore them with aplomb. The clarity of her teachings completely won over the Fillmores.

In the April 1890 issue of Charles' magazine a student described one of Mrs. Hopkins' lectures on her second visit to Kansas City. According to the report, during the lecture "long tongues of flame shot out from her vicinity and filled the room with a rosy light that continued throughout the remainder of the lecture to roll over the class in waves and ripples of what seemed golden sunlight. Many saw it plainly while others sensed its uplifting presence in the room." Today this report does not seem too startling; there are many people who are sensitive to such phenomena and describe them in similar terms.

At any rate, best of all, Charles and Myrtle found in Mrs. Hopkins an understanding friend—a rare gift in this world. It is even more unusual to find such friendship in the high realm of metaphysical teachers. Intimacy and warmth between teachers in the metaphysical and occult world, and between teachers and their students, is as rare as a Koh-i-noor in the world of jewels. Charles and Myrtle found the friendship of Emma Curtis Hopkins a blessing throughout their lives.

The importance of this event has eluded many authors who have written about Charles Fillmore. They report the technical fact that he had little "formal schooling," but fail to emphasize his years of tutorship as a teenager under the guidance of Mrs. Edgar Taylor in St. Cloud. The same casual treatment is given to Charles Fillmore's study under Emma Curtis Hopkins.

It is well to recognize that good tutoring can do as much for a good student as formal schooling—if not more. Emma Curtis Hopkins was a superb teacher, and she taught Charles how to use his far-reaching mind so as to coordinate the essential teachings of many spiritual traditions.

One who knew Emma Curtis Hopkins writes: "Mrs. Hopkins' gift for teaching showed itself early. Before she was fifteen years old she entered Woodstock Academy [Connecticut] as a student and because of her genius was given a place on the faculty as a teacher."*

The words of Emma Curtis Hopkins rang harmoniously in Charles Fillmore's ears because she spoke of Christ. When Charles found Christ he found himself.

At that time many teachers were using the term "Christian Science" to describe the new metaphysics. Indeed, at the time he started his magazine, in the second issue of *Modern Thought,* Charles explained his use of the term, saying "By Christian Science, we mean all metaphysical schools." In 1891 Charles accordingly changed the name of his magazine to *Christian Science Thought.* Some time after this change Mary Baker Eddy took the stand that the words "Christian Science" belonged exclusively to her. Charles dropped these words from the magazine in 1892, keeping the title: *Thought.*

In the meantime, other unfolding ideas impelled Charles and Myrtle to new activities. Myrtle was now co-editor, with a special department in her charge named "Society of Silent Help."

---

*Emma Curtis Hopkins, *Introduction to Scientific Christian Mental Practice.*

Here was an idea of such import that there is no human mensuration to gauge its worth. For out of the Society of Silent Help emerged Silent Unity. The heart of the Unity movement today is Silent Unity, that department of dedicated prayer which responds annually to a million appeals for prayer.

The formation of the Society of Silent Help brought a widespread instantaneous response. Something far more potent than the publication of a magazine was flowing into expression. An inspiration that would lead to far greater issues was streaming into the minds and hearts of the Fillmores. What fruitage it would produce they did not know at the time, for their project was only a year old.

Myrtle said in her announcement of the Society of Silent Help: "A little band in this city have agreed to meet in silent communion every night at ten o'clock all those who are in trouble, sickness, or poverty, and who sincerely desire the help of the Good Father."

Carrying out their own instructions, Charles and Myrtle met with a few friends in their home every night to pray and to help all who turned to them in thought.

With the next issue of the magazine Myrtle announced that the time of silent prayer would be changed from 10:00 to 9:00 every night. "Persons living in the country," she wrote, "have written us that they should like to become members but were prevented by the lateness of the hour of communion."

In September 1890 Charles moved his publication offices to the Hall Building, Ninth and Walnut Streets. At last, a year and a half after publication, they were able to hire a typesetter for the magazine. There were three rooms in the new location. The typesetter used one room, and the other two rooms became offices for the editors and for visitors. They always had visitors! Charles invited people in constantly and Myrtle always welcomed them with friendliness and warmth.

Actually the two offices were not separated as there was an archway between them. One office held desks; the other had chairs for class meetings. For Sunday meetings the Knights of Pythias hall in the same building was used. It began to emerge that meetings were also important, and Charles and Myrtle became the group leaders.

At first the meetings were informal. Charles, who loved to sing, would start with a hymn. Then he would answer questions, even propound a few for the group, and Myrtle would lead in prayer. Discussions followed. Friends returned to the meetings and brought others—proof that their spiritual needs were being met.

The group eventually became too large and too varied for discussion, and Charles began to deliver an address on Sunday. Myrtle would guide the meditation with suitable words of prayer.

Charles began to express his talent as a speaker and leader. His talks were simple but profound discourses, not sermons. He prayed in a direct manner that touched the hearts of his hearers, awakening in them a new understanding of God's presence and power.

Eric Butterworth, minister of the New York City Unity Center of Practical Christianity, says, "Charles Fillmore taught me how to pray. He never addressed God to give Him information. He never informed God that it was Sunday, or Wednesday, or a holiday of some kind. He never told God that we were all gathered together to worship Him, and so forth. He assumed that God knew all that. He would affirm God's presence and power. He would gratefully acknowledge God's gifts and providence. He awakened us to God's presence."

In December 1890 Charles and Myrtle attended a class meeting of Emma Curtis Hopkins' students in Chicago. For ten days they took part with one hundred and twenty students in the work of the seminary—class work, lectures, meditation, and prayer. They basked in the sunlight of Mrs. Hopkins' teachings.

During this visit C. I. Thacher, a student of Mrs. Hopkins, held a party in his home for the group. The party was enlivened by an orchestra and by dancing. Myrtle tells an amusing story about

Charles, who rushed into the middle of the floor at one point during the festivities and shouted, "I can't dance but I can sing. Let's sing!"

What did Charles invite them to sing? "Praise God from Whom All Blessings Flow." Myrtle says the house shook with the hymn, which they sang without benefit of music from the orchestra. Myrtle adds, "The musicians looked funny."

The Fillmores invited Mrs. Hopkins to return to Kansas City, as did the Thachers, and Mrs. Hopkins subsequently came to Kansas City several times.

While Charles and Myrtle were in Chicago, Grandma Fillmore, ever quietly in the background, took care of Lowell, Rick, and Royal.

Rosemary Fillmore Rhea, daughter of Rickert Fillmore, told me that her father had said to her several times, "In those days Grandma not only cooked, but sewed for us. Once she took some old draperies and made clothes for me and Uncle Lowell. During this period Charles Fillmore wore suits which had been given to him, and often they had to be altered to fit him properly."

In spite of this necessary economy Charles would not set a price for counseling services or for the work of Silent Unity. There was a nominal charge for the magazine because of postal regulations, but even that was waived for those who could not pay. It was not an easy time. In later years Charles would say with characteristic understatement, "The way has not always been strewn with roses."

Here and there, however, in certain of Charles' remarks the conditions may be discerned. He always gave credit to Myrtle for his ability to stand firm.

"Once," said Charles, "when our finances were low and I was almost ready to give up the love-offering plan, Myrtle encouraged me to hold out. 'This is the right way,' she declared. 'God will support us in it. He will carry us through to success if we follow as He leads us.' "

Charles worked far into the nights, not only as editor, but also as a writer for the magazine *Thought*. Because he was still in the real-estate business and his associates ridiculed his new activities, he wrote under the pen name of "Leo-Virgo." The title was adroit as Charles was born on August 22, when the sun was leaving the sign of Leo and entering the sign of Virgo. He used the title until he was no longer in business and was devoting his whole time to metaphysical work.

No matter how busy they were, the Fillmores never failed to hold the nightly meetings of the Society of Silent Help in their own home. At one of these meetings in the spring of 1891 when they were sitting in the silence, Charles suddenly exclaimed, "UNITY! That's it. UNITY!" Charles' friends, surprised by his unusual disruption of the silence, wondered what was going on.

"UNITY!" cried Charles again. "That's the name of our work! That's the name we've been looking for!"

So might Archimedes have shouted "Eureka!" In that moment Unity, the movement, was born.

9 "First the Blade"

Now that the name Unity was established, the Society of Silent Help was renamed the Society of Silent Unity. The shortened term Silent Unity soon came into use, however, and today, more than eighty years later, this name is known all over the world.

There are some ideas which come so immediately into fruit that the fruitage may be called a precipitation. Silent Unity was a spiritual precipitation which made the work of prayer supremely important in the movement.

The magazine announcement of Silent Unity with instructions for those who wished to start meetings for prayer brought floods of letters. Soon there were hundreds of people in small groups joining Silent Unity at nine in the evening.

At that time Charles and Myrtle were the only workers at headquarters. Yet busy as they were they invited readers who needed prayer to write letters giving brief details regarding their needs. Of course it was not possible for the Fillmores to answer all these letters, but they assured the writers that Silent Unity would be praying for them.

Often Charles would not go to bed until dawn. To others who were up before him he would say with a humorous gleam in his eyes, "As you see, I am a late sleeper."

Charles developed the ability to do without much sleep, but he also developed the habit of taking catnaps during the day and in the evening. They lasted for only a few moments, during which he closed his eyes as if he had withdrawn into the silence for meditation. He would close his eyes, even on a platform during meetings, and there were times when his friends were not sure whether he was catnapping or going into the silence. Sometimes there were amusing consequences, for later he would show by his remarks that he had heard everything that was going on while his eyes were closed.

Charles decided to publish another magazine as a special organ for the Society of Silent Unity. It was called *Unity,* and contained appropriate articles on prayer, many reprinted from *Thought.* The magazine *Thought* was still being published, so the Fillmores had two magazines to edit.

A winged globe, today the well-known symbol of Unity, appeared on the first issue of the new magazine in June 1891. It attracted much interest because of the way Charles explained its symbolism. "It is a symbol that I feel I knew in a former incarnation in ancient Egypt," he declared.

The statement startled many students. In the 1890s such a declaration was sure to disturb the climate of orthodox belief. Those who had any sympathy with the idea of reincarnation did not speak of it unless they were theosophists or occultists. At that time it was regarded as a non-Christian belief; to declare oneself a believer in reincarnation was tantamount to declaring oneself a non-Christian.

Here was Charles Fillmore, the founder of a movement based on the teachings of Jesus Christ, expounding reincarnation! It was an act of courage, and yet characteristically for Charles it was simply a frank statement. Today in the Christian world there are many thousands —perhaps millions—who accept reincarnation as a reasonable hypothesis in spite of their theological pundits, but at the end of the last century it was a "far-out" concept.

In his explanation of the winged globe Charles went on to say, "It represents the relation between Spirit, soul, and body. Back of the soul is Spirit, which quickens and energizes the soul, that is, gives the soul wings."

Charles had more to say. He outlined a most profound esoteric tradition and showed himself far more deeply versed in the ancient wisdom than his simple words implied. "The winged globe is also a symbol of the earth and its soul. The earth has soul, as have its products of every description. All exist in the ether, the *anima mundi,* the divine mother. When the people of the earth lift up their thoughts to God, the *Animus Dei* or directive Spirit, then the planet takes wings into a higher radiation of universal life—the mortal puts on immortality."

Charles changed the name of his publication firm to the "Unity Book Company" when the magazine *Unity* was published. Within a short time, however, he changed the name again to the "Unity Tract Society."

"We have adopted the word 'tract,' " Charles announced, "because it is a synonym of religious literature issued without the idea of gain. This is not a business but a ministry."

Still the economic situation was not easy. Money was going out as fast as it was coming in. Great faith was needed, great staying power, and constant prayer. It was during this period that Charles and Myrtle signed a "Covenant" between them, a covenant expressing their own mutual agreement to stand fast at any cost and to dedicate their all to Unity. They told no one of this "letter to God." It was "laid away" and hidden from human eyes until it was discovered among Myrtle's papers in 1942, eleven years after her death.

Dedication and Covenant

We, Charles Fillmore and Myrtle Fillmore, husband and wife, hereby dedicate ourselves, our time, our money, all we have and all we expect to have, to the Spirit of Truth, and through it, to the Society of Silent Unity.

It being understood and agreed that the said Spirit of Truth shall render unto us an equivalent for this dedication, in peace of mind, health of body, wisdom, understanding, love, life and an abundant supply of all things necessary to meet every want without our making any of these things the object of our existence.

In the presence of the Conscious Mind of Christ Jesus, this 7th day of December A.D. 1892.

Charles Fillmore
Myrtle Fillmore

In *Myrtle Fillmore's Healing Letters* there is a letter to a friend in which she says: "I suggest that you write a letter to God, telling, putting into words, that which your heart holds and hopes for. Have faith that God is seeing your letter and your heart, and that there is wisdom and power and freedom and love to accomplish that which will meet your needs."

Myrtle gave her friend this advice because, as she had said in a preceding sentence, "Sometimes I have written a letter to God and laid it away, in the assurance that the eyes of the loving and all-wise Father were seeing my letter and knowing my heart and working to find ways to bless me and help me grow."

Those who know the stringent economic circumstances at the time the Covenant was written can truly appreciate the faith expressed in this "letter to God."

In August 1893, Myrtle brought the magazine *Wee Wisdom* into being. The first issue was a paper of eight pages with a subscription price of fifty cents a year. This was below the cost of publication, and it is noteworthy that the price today is still below cost. *Wee Wisdom* is the oldest children's magazine in the country, and throughout the years it has been supported by the Unity movement. *Wee Wisdom* is also issued free in Braille.

For thirty years Myrtle remained the editor, also contributing stories, articles, and poems. The magazine was one of her pet projects since it was the fulfillment of a need which had appeared to her in a dramatic vision. In her vision Myrtle saw a great crowd of people, most of them children, rushing, pushing, scrambling, and piling over one another. She was able to watch the turmoil in this vision as if she were viewing a moving picture, at the same time feeling great concern for the children.

"Who will take care of the children?" she asked. In her vision she was impelled by some power to the front of the crowd, and she heard a voice saying, "You are to take care of the children. This is your work."

Thus Unity has never considered *Wee Wisdom* a money-making activity and has supported the magazine as a project of inestimable spiritual value. For similar reasons the Sunday school has always been considered of great importance in Unity. It was started in the earliest days by Myrtle, and today the Sunday school teachers continue in inspired succession to fulfill the task undertaken by her.

The World's Parliament of Religions, the first of its kind, was held in Chicago during the World's Columbian Exposition in 1893. Representatives of all religions gathered in amity to expound their teachings and to engage in discussion. That summer Charles and Myrtle Fillmore attended the congress held in Chicago by New Thought adherents as part of the World's Parliament of Religions.

The exposition, celebrating the four-hundredth anniversary of the discovery of America by Christopher Columbus, was said to be the finest ever held in the world up to that time. The most prominent personages in America came to the opening ceremonies. The architecture, colossal, symmetric, and decorative, was to influence architectural style in America for years. The religious leaders at the congress were chosen by the various administrators of the great world religions, so that as a religious event it should have been of great consequence. The promise of ecumenism, however, was not fulfilled.

Philosophically, it is interesting to note that after the World's Parliament of Religions dispersed, two movements regarded by theologians as "cults" began to gain ground. It is still more significant that both of these movements had to do with the concept of Oneness. They were Unity and Vedanta. Unity regards the essence of all true religion as One. Vedanta teaches the absolute Oneness of all Being.

It was at the World's Parliament of Religions that Swami Vivekananda, and through him Vedanta, became popularly known. Swami Vivekananda came from India to attend the congress, winning the hearts of so many supporters that he was encouraged to remain and to establish centers for the dissemination of Ramakrishna's message. He formed groups, lectured, and wrote books which brought the teachings of Vedanta to the American public. From that time the fine distinctions and analytical nuances of Vedanta have attracted knowledgeable students in America.

The leaders of the great world religions came to Chicago, read from their scripts, and departed, but little that they said proved important to orthodox religious history. Few among the speakers would later stir the hearts of men.

Today, eight decades later, we can see how significant it was that out of the grand array of theological potentates at the Columbian Exposition two men would become important—neither of them theologians. One of them was Swami Vivekananda, a simple monk of the Ramakrishna Order; the other was Charles Fillmore. Both men always spoke from their hearts.

Back in Kansas City, Charles and Myrtle spent much time working on their magazines. Myrtle continued a serial for children which she had started with the first issue of *Wee Wisdom*. She would read her story to Lowell, then eleven years old, and accept his corrections when he said, "Mother, boys don't say it that way!" As a result, the story, in hard-cover, proved to be one of the most popular books published by Unity.

In the course of her versatile reading, Myrtle discovered a booklet, "Finding the Christ in Ourselves," by a homeopathic physician in New York, H. Emilie Cady. She passed it on to Charles, who liked it so much that he invited Dr. Cady to write for *Unity*. A few articles by Dr. Cady began to appear in January 1892. But Charles felt that a consecutive, progressive series of lessons would be more important than occasional articles, and he requested Dr. Cady to write such a series. Dr. Cady, a pupil of Emma Curtis Hopkins, gladly consented.

Here again Charles showed his genius as an editor. Of greater importance, however, is the fact that Charles was beginning to express his gift of encouraging talent in others. Today, some twenty-five years after his death, those who remember Charles Fillmore say that this gift was one of his greatest and most endearing qualities. Not only did he help those around him to discover their talent, but he also nourished those talents and brought them to flower.

Whenever I have talked to those who knew Charles Fillmore I have seen a deep feeling of gratitude in their eyes as they speak of his friendship. I have heard in their voices a warmth which has spanned the years and has made me feel in touch with the grace of Charles Fillmore.

Lowell Fillmore; Charles Rickert Fillmore, Charles' grandson; Rosemary, his granddaughter; May Rowland; Ernest C. Wilson; L. E. Meyer; James Dillet Freeman; Vera Dawson Tait; Richard Lynch; Eric Butterworth and others, all speak of Charles Fillmore with profound gratitude. Add to these friends all who were encouraged in their generation and have passed on, and Charles Fillmore appears as a spiritual artist whose creative medium was the human heart.

Just as important, moreover, is the fact that a similar influence was exerted by Myrtle Fillmore. Even as they were co-founders of the movement, so were Myrtle and Charles co-developers of human potentiality. Myrtle's friendship is remembered personally with the same depth of affection.

The Fillmores attended the annual session of the International

Divine Science Association in Chicago in 1895, and there they were glad to have some influence in persuading the group to meet in Kansas City in 1896. They committed themselves heartily to this association meeting, arranging board and lodging in Kansas City for visitors and attending to their needs. Board and lodging for a whole week cost four dollars a person in those days, and it was good board in good rooms with good meals.

In 1898 Charles purchased a house at 1315 McGee Street in order to obtain larger headquarters for Unity. The seed of Unity was sprouting a young blade. "First the blade, then the ear, after that the full corn in the ear" (Mark 4:28).

10 "Then the Ear"

The new headquarters on McGee Street was a two-story brick house
set back from the street on a high terrace. On both sides of the house
were wide porches covered with vines, and shade trees graced the
ample grounds.

On the first floor were two large rooms separated by folding doors.
During the week these rooms were used for offices, and on Sundays
the doors folded back to form a large meeting room. Folding chairs
seated one hundred people.

A period of happy expansion followed. As ever, financial income
and outgo were equal, but the time of stringent poverty had given
way to a moderate flow of funds. True, there was neither luxury nor
surplus money, but there was right growth. Those who now sur-
rounded Charles and Myrtle at headquarters were true friends and
helpers.

Here indeed was a rare circumstance, for friendship and leadership were combined as they seldom are in the history of spiritual
movements. Usually a movement follows what seems a foreordained
human pattern. First, a leader with a strong mind and an attractive
personality forms a group around him. His word is regarded as
"holy" and soon comes to be looked on as a revelation which his
followers deem the only path to holiness, redemption, freedom,

heaven, or some experience of glory. Very seldom is there true intimacy between the leader and the followers, though there may be much glamorous devotion. In the course of time the gap widens between the holy or inspired leader and his followers.

As for the followers themselves, there is usually high spiritual competiveness among them for the favor of the leader and for some kind of appointment as a supernumerary. True friendship in such groups is rare.

Not only are true friendship and radiant warmth missing, but the dominant mind of the leader usually inhibits original thought in the group. As a result, when the leader dies, the group often splits into factions and the original inspiration fades away.

Again and again I have seen this pattern of group growth and of group loss in the metaphysical and occult field. Such a pattern obeys a human law of limitation, through which the dominance of the superior and the submission of the inferiors prove harmful in the end. Rare indeed is the leader who leads without leading. Rare indeed is the leader who inspires others in such a way that the inspiration appears to them as their own. Rare indeed is the leader who is a friend to his followers and the center of a group of participating friends.

At this stage of Unity Charles and Myrtle were forming the nucleus of such a group. It was a most important time because they were establishing a movement in which leadership would be guidance, not dominance, a movement in which work would be carried on through inspiration shared by everyone in the group.

This time of growth at McGee Street brought faithful workers who proved to be staunch friends. Business activities continued to expand. At the rear of the house was the composing room, where two women worked at typesetting. Four staff workers occupied the office close to the composing room.

The parlor was used as Charles Fillmore's office. At nine o'clock in the morning when Charles came to the office there were several persons waiting in the reception room to see him. All day long he saw these people, gave them counsel, prayed with them, inspired them.

Charles was in his mid-forties, at what some people would call the peak of maturity. He denied the word "peak" in that phrase; he maintained that a high plateau of health and vigor was possible for man, without any descending valley of decrepitude. There was but little limp in his walk; his leg was no longer shriveled, but strong and full.

Callers saw a slender man of medium height, with a wiry frame and a neatly trimmed beard. His face was serene, and his friendly blue eyes conveyed a deep interest in the visitor. His face might light up suddenly with a quick smile, or his eyes might close for a few moments as he turned inward in prayer.

Whenever he was asked about his counseling methods, Charles often said, "It seems to me that I say very little."

This "little" healed, however, and more and more people flocked to McGee Street to see him. Pain-racked callers found release from pain and freedom from fear. So-called incurable diseases, Charles informed his callers, could be cured by God; "incurable" referred to the doctor's knowledge, not to God's wisdom and power.

Later Lowell Fillmore would say, "On McGee Street father did most of the healing." Charles himself never spoke of these cures, and others heard of them only through the people who had been healed, or their relatives and friends. Some of the cases have found their way into Unity's archives.

James Dillet Freeman in his *Household of Faith* records a number of incidents. One woman telephoned Charles in great distress the night before she was to undergo an operation for a tumor. After her conversation with Charles she fell asleep and slept well for the first time in many weeks. The next morning when the doctors examined her the tumor had disappeared.

Another woman with tuberculosis of the lungs was told that she had only a short time to live. A few months later she reported to Charles, "I am now strong and healthy and doing my own housework."

This woman's husband was also healed after she wired Charles for help, reporting that surgeons in a hospital despaired of his life. He had been operated on for a strangulated hernia which had poisoned his system. In four days the wound was healed and the man was well.

Another healing with interesting aspects came as a result of class instruction. A state legislator, a diabetic, enrolled in one of Charles Fillmore's classes in Truth. During the fourth session he suddenly had the conviction that he was healed. His assurance was noteworthy because the legislator had been refused insurance and had been told that he had an advanced case of diabetes. In one month his weight increased from ninety-two pounds to one hundred and thirty pounds. He was able to discard his rigid diet, and tests revealed that the diabetes had disappeared.

Yet this was not all. For seventeen years he had had a withered right arm, one inch shorter than the left. One day he was astonished to find that the right arm had returned to its original length and usefulness.

In spite of all his counseling and writing, Charles found time for a full social and family life. He loved picnics; the Fourth of July and St. Valentine's Day were favorite picnic holidays. At those gala events about two hundred people turned out to picnic in Budd Park. Thanksgiving and Christmas also meant parties, with Charles telling jokes, singing, reciting, and encouraging others to join in the fun.

Charles' love of dramatic recitation caused him to shave his beard for a performance at one of the events. He had decided to act out the story of an Irish washerwoman who was trying to get her little boy a job, taking him along with her for personal appeal. "I looked all right dressed up for the part," said Charles, "but who would think I was a washerwoman with a beard? So I shaved my beard off."

This new beardlessness was a surprise to some of the subscribers of *Unity*. When a picture of the headquarters staff was published in *Unity* and Charles appeared clean-shaven, a subscriber wrote in, "If cutting off your beard makes you look like that in the picture, I hope you will let it grow again."

Lunchtime at McGee Street was a group affair. One of the workers prepared a hot dish or two on the kitchen stove, and all would eat at a large table. Because Charles and Myrtle advocated vegetarianism, the meals were meatless. Staff workers found the simple lunch so much to their liking that they also embraced vegetarianism. From this simple beginning Unity Inn would later emerge.

At times there came to headquarters certain visitors who were not so deeply interested in Truth as they were in free board and lodging. So that the rooms upstairs at McGee Street could be used for guests, the Fillmores lived elsewhere, on Elmwood Avenue.

Rosemary Fillmore Rhea tells a story of those early days which she heard from her father, Rickert. Since Rick himself was about fourteen or fifteen his memory was no doubt enhanced by details heard from the family.

On one occasion a guest who remained in bed and claimed to be ill was treated by a doctor, to no avail. Finally the doctor announced his next treatment in solemn tones. "If you are not better," he said, "next time I will have to give you a special cold-water treatment. We will fill a tub with ice water—it will be cold enough to have ice floating in it—and immerse you thoroughly in the tub. It is a certain cure for your disease."

The next time the doctor called his patient had vanished. Friendship of the Fillmore family with the doctor is another indication of Charles' practical and common-sense approach to the healing of disease at a time when some metaphysicians were scornful of *materia medica*.

Yet Charles did not seek doctors or medical treatment for himself. James Dillet Freeman tells the story of an event many years later, when Charles and some other persons were involved in an automobile accident. When the doctor came up to attend to him, Charles said, in spite of pain, "Just leave me alone, I'll do this my own way."

"Ah!" said the doctor, respecting his request. "There is a man."

Charles Fillmore's recovery from the accident was prompt and complete.

When Lowell Fillmore graduated from high school he went to work at Unity headquarters. His pay was five dollars a week, and what he did for this amount would astonish high school graduates today who work for ten times that salary. Lowell ran the small job press. He took the heavy forms from the composing room and drove them in a hired wagon to the printer. As the printing shop was some distance away, the operation was a delicate one, involving care not to "pie" or break up the delicate alignment of the forms. It was also a task demanding strength. Subsequently Lowell brought the forms back to McGee Street. He then cut brown paper wrappers for the magazines and mailed them, checking to make sure that new subscribers received their issues.

With the dawn of the new century the Unity movement showed heartening signs of growth. The year 1900 was filled with enthusiastic prophecies from all quarters regarding the future of the nation. A dynamic optimism was in the air. That year the Democratic National Convention was held in Kansas City, nominating William Jennings Bryan for president. Kansas City business was on the upturn again, and the city as well as the state looked forward to greater prosperity than ever.

At the time Charles began to hold a series of summer classes in Pueblo and Denver. Charles always liked to return to Colorado. He liked mountains. They represented for him "exaltation, a high plane of consciousness, a state of spiritual realization." This definition of "mountain" in *The Metaphysical Bible Dictionary* of Unity expresses Charles' feeling about the mountains of the Great Continental Divide.

The Colorado Summer School of Metaphysics was held in Manitou in August 1901. It was an outdoor school, with classes held in a large tent. Surrounding this tent were smaller tents for the students, the teachers, and the Fillmores. Grandma Fillmore was there, cooking (as usual) in the Fillmore tent and keeping an eye on the boys.

Back at McGee Street that fall, Unity meetings became so popular that the room seating a hundred people became inadequate. A large hall had to be rented elsewhere. By 1902 there were six workers at headquarters to help Charles and Myrtle answer letters written to Silent Unity for advice and prayer.

Individual counseling and healing now took so many hours of the day that the Fillmores had little time to guide the movement. Reluctantly, they decided not to spend so much time counseling, though they never gave up the practice completely. So Charles and Myrtle trained counselors and helped them to take over the personal healing work. Myrtle remained in charge, and every morning at ten o'clock she led this group in a healing meeting which started their day.

Subscribers were calling on Charles to write a book. He replied, "I wish to attain such command of my organism that I can demonstrate what I write."

There is startling honesty in this reply. Charles had discovered that there was advanced spiritual work for him to do, and he set about doing it, developing a technique which he would teach in later years. He had proved that he could work for hours on end far into the night, but there was a higher demonstration to be made. He drilled himself in certain techniques which he worked out step by step. He felt that he owed his students this kind of presentation—what else could be expected from a School of Practical Christianity?

Leadership in any form makes a demand on the leader. However selfless the group surrounding a spiritual leader may be, there is an interplay of thought, a silent seeking on the part of the group which every sensitive leader feels. The group surrounding Charles and Myrtle was selfless, but who can declare there was no pull, no effect which Charles could sense? The mass consciousness of the human race has many side effects, and sometimes the side effect of advancing age plays upon the leader's consciousness. It may be no more than the awareness of accumulating years in the face of a responsible task, but this awareness must sooner or later be faced.

At such a time the pressure of the group and the piling up of years coalesce and the leader has to find a transcendent source of strength. Sometimes the leader has to adopt a new mode of life, or climb to new heights of inspiration, or develop a new technique, in order to master the situation. Charles did not take up a new mode of life, but he climbed to new heights of prayer and developed a technique which has been of inestimable value to his students. Charles always spoke of this stage with his usual frankness.

"I was nearing the half-century mark," he said, "and I began to get wrinkled and gray, my knees tottered, and a great weakness came over me."

This from Charles! "Then," he said, "I went deep down within my body and talked to the inner life-centers. I told them with firmness and decision that I would never submit to the old-age devil, that I was determined never to give in. Gradually, I felt a new life current coming up from the life-center. It was a faint little stream at first, and months went by before I got it to the surface. Now it is growing strong by leaps and bounds. My cheeks have filled out, the wrinkles and crow's feet are gone, and I actually feel like the boy I am."

Charles was always honest. His statement that months went by is a frank admission that should give heart to those who find themselves faced with the same problem in a busy world. He did not retreat from the world nor from his family and friends, but established his mastery in the midst of events.

"By silently affirming my unity with the infinite energy of the one true God," Charles said, "I gained renewed youthfulness and power."

In 1902, when Charles found it necessary to rent a larger hall for meetings, he persuaded his staff to form a building committee.

"Wouldn't it be wonderful," he asked, "if we could find a place —or build one—where we can house all our activities under one roof?"

On July 29, 1903, Charles incorporated the Unity Society of Practical Christianity in Kansas City, taking great care not to found it as a sectarian church, but as a "society for scientific and educational purposes, viz.: the study and demonstration of universal law." Today the Unity Society of Practical Christianity remains a distinct organization of Truth students in Kansas City, owning Unity Temple on Country Club Plaza.

In the meantime Charles began to envision new headquarters, a building or a location where all the activities of Unity could be carried on. In 1905, after they had worked at McGee Street for seven years, he felt that the time for greater expansion had come. Though they had no funds, Charles was sure the money would be forthcoming.

A building committee had been formed in 1901 but no action had been taken. One member at the initial meeting had humorously offered a cent as the first contribution. Charles blandly accepted the cent and blessed it. In 1903 the fund had twenty-five cents; now in 1905, $601. Charles said, "Let's go ahead."

The building committee finally found an eight-room house with a large lot for sale at 913 Tracy Avenue. Charles said, "Let's buy!"

There was no money, but at that moment Unity's new headquarters came into being "in the ether of the Kingdom of the heavens."

11 The Tracy Avenue Headquarters

The down payment demanded for the parcel of land at 913 Tracy Avenue was several times greater than the total of six hundred dollars in the building fund. In addition, still more money would be needed for alterations to the house on the lot. It was a time of fervent prayer for the Fillmores and for the building committee. The directors of the Unity Society pledged a hundred dollars each, but this was a mere beginning.

One evening while they were gathered in prayer, Daniel Hoagland, a member of the board, rose from his seat and said, "I believe in the ideas of Unity. For several years I have been attending these meetings, and I have been inspired by the teachings of the Fillmores. I cannot help but have the same kind of faith that they have. It is important for this faith, and the ideas of Unity, to be carried to as many as possible. So I will provide funds for the purchase of the lot and for the erection of a building."

There was a murmur of surprise, particularly because Daniel Hoagland was not a rich man.

"I am not wealthy, as you know," he continued, sensing the cause of their surprise. "I have a wife and four little children to provide for, but I will mortgage my home to provide the money needed to start this project. I have confidence that I will be repaid."

Before the mortgage was obtained some of Daniel Hoagland's business friends tried to discourage him, asserting that Unity was not a good financial risk.

But Unity's benefactor would not be dissuaded, and he obtained the money for the purchase of the property. Of course he was ultimately repaid. In later years Daniel Hoagland's daughter May Rowland would devote her life to Silent Unity as its director.

The house at 913 Tracy Avenue was moved to the rear of the lot for the use of the headquarters staff. Soon a vegetarian cafeteria of humble proportions was started on the ground floor since most of the workers were vegetarians and liked to eat together. The cafeteria was to become Unity Inn as its popularity increased.

The down payment for the lot and the cost of moving the house to the rear had almost depleted their funds, but Charles Fillmore's faith was strong. He gave orders to proceed with the building of the printing plant and administrative offices. In the meantime *Unity* magazine asked subscribers for contributions.

The building was started in September 1905 and eleven months later, on August 19, 1906, hundreds of Unity students from all parts of the country came to Kansas City to celebrate the laying of the cornerstone. The building, three stories high, contained a printing plant, offices, a large reception room, a chapel seating more than two hundred, and an upper room, a sanctuary of healing for Unity workers. In this room lights burned day and night, forecasting the ever-illumined Silent Unity window in Unity Village today, a prayer-beacon well known to millions throughout the United States and abroad.

Two months later Charles attended the convention of the International New Thought Federation in Chicago. The federation, however, was not ready for any constitution, and there were so many diverse opinions that Charles decided he could not give it his support.

"The name 'New Thought,' " Charles declared, "has been appropriated by so many cults with new theories that it has ceased to express what I conceive to be absolute Truth."

So Charles decided that Unity would go its way, based on his original platform of a practical Christianity. He was characteristically frank.

"I have decided that I am no longer a New Thoughter," he added. "I have a standard of faith which is true and logical, and I must conform to it in my teaching without compromise. We call it Practical Christianity, and under this name we shall henceforth do our work."

This statement caused a flurry in New Thought circles. Many people were surprised, yet Charles was following his fundamental line of logic and he was being true to his original vision.

Outspoken though he was, Charles remained a good friend of many New Thought leaders. It is heartening to find that many New Thought lecturers who came to Kansas City later were entertained by Charles and Myrtle Fillmore. Moreover, they were invited to speak before the Unity Society and were graciously and warmly welcomed.

The Unity movement kept on growing. In 1910 an even larger building was erected on the adjoining lot at 917 Tracy Avenue. In September of that year the printing plant was moved to the new building, which was large enough to take care of the three magazines *Unity, Wee Wisdom,* and a recent addition, *Weekly Unity.*

Weekly Unity first appeared on May 15, 1909, with Lowell Fillmore as editor. Lowell had filled every conceivable job on the magazines *Modern Thought* and *Unity.* He was now twenty-seven years old, and the new task suited him to perfection.

Charles created another department of Unity in 1909: He inaugurated the Correspondence School. Many magazine subscribers and people who had been healed through the prayers of Silent Unity were asking for a curriculum of some kind. For some time he had been thinking of establishing a correspondence course, but he had been too busy. Charles himself knew a great deal about such matters.

Sometimes when he was asked whether he knew anything about correspondence courses, a twinkle would come into his eyes and he would say, "Well, I have taken more than forty correspondence courses. And some of them cost $100 apiece."

When Charles established his course, he asked no payment for it, saying that he would send it out on the freewill offering plan.

"I finally decided to take action," he said, "when someone wrote asking us to send her immediately the first lesson in our correspondence course. It was one of those faith demands that cannot go unrewarded! The faith in her letter quickened my faith."

Charles' method of work is well exemplified in the way he took action. "I formulated an agreement and sent it to her to sign. I wrote the first lesson in the meantime, and when the signed agreement was returned, the lesson was ready to be mailed."

And yet, above and beyond all this, the ready response of Charles in this instance indicates the way he worked and guided Unity. For Charles himself the competence that others saw was the result of prayer. Unity was growing, not because of his personal planning, but because of spiritual vision and faith. The outward growth was the result of inner vision; such growth would always be right and safe.

The Unity Correspondence School enrolled two thousand students within two years. Since its establishment it has taught a great many thousands of students. Today, through a process of transformation, its curriculum is a part of the Unity Institute of Continuing Education.

Not only did Charles write Unity's first correspondence course in 1909, but he also completed his first book, *Christian Healing.* Twenty years after the publication of his first issue of *Modern Thought*—twenty years during which he had written editorials and hundreds of articles for the magazines, taught innumerable classes, given countless lectures—his first book appeared.

Christian Healing emphasized the principles on which he based his life. Three years had passed since he had made his stand among New Thought leaders for the recognition of the Christ-principle, and discussion in the field since then caused him to reaffirm his vision.

Many vital questions concerning Christ were agitating the world anew at this period of history. The theological dogmas regarding Christ had become outworn for intelligent seekers who could not subscribe to the narrow sectarianism of the times—each sect claiming its own concept of the Christ as the sole truth and the only approach to salvation. In the realm of metaphysics and of New Thought a non-dogmatic idea of Christ was emerging, but not yet was the idea clear or potent.

Charles Fillmore's emphatic and firm statement would have an effect later on the New Thought movement, but in the meantime like Luther he was taking his stand. Not to a theological hierarchy, but to an *omnium gatherum* of religious innovators, he was saying, "Here I stand, I can do no else. For me Christ is central."

Charles Fillmore was not the only teacher at the time to emphasize the importance of Christ. As early as 1886, three years before Charles published his first issue of *Modern Thought*, Warren Felt Evans was expressing a similar idea regarding the nature of the Christ in his book *Esoteric Christianity and Mental Therapeutics*. At about the same time Emma Curtis Hopkins was founding her seminary in Chicago, and her parallel ideas regarding Christ were accepted by many of her students.

But Charles was advancing beyond this stage. He was taking the next step: He was announcing himself a personal disciple of Christ.

In London at about the same time in 1909 another teacher was also calling attention to the centrality of Christ. Judge Thomas Troward had just begun to lecture and to write, having retired to England after a life devoted to jurisprudence in India. As his lectures developed and became popular and his books increased in number, his masterful development of New Thought principles greatly influenced the New Thought movement in the British Isles.

In his works Judge Troward with keen legal genius presented Christ as the central figure of divine manifestation. Reasoning along lines of spiritual logic, he so won the hearts and minds of his hearers that the British New Thought movement accepted this recognition of Christ as logical. The development, however, was only beginning, and its fruition was yet to come.

In another realm of religious innovation a similar struggle was also taking place, with agony for a proponent who insisted on the central-ity of Christ. The occult world in Europe was shaken when Rudolph Steiner withdrew from the Theosophical movement because, as he declared, it lacked Christocentric emphasis. Steiner's withdrawal was to take place in 1913, but it is significant to find at this period the world-wide emergence of a more universal idea regarding Christ, free from theological dogmas and sectarian claims.

It would be another ten years before another writer in the esoteric field, Alice Bailey, would also appear to emphasize the centrality of the Christ. Her twenty-four books would include a masterly presenta-tion of the World-Christ as a central figure, guiding and aiding human evolution on our planet.

For students with a world view of human thought it is significant that talented teachers in newborn religious fields at this period were independently coming to the conclusion that the old theological dogmas regarding Christ were inadequate for the twentieth century. In their own idioms these teachers would declare emphatically that there is a World-Christ whose divine function is the guidance of the human race on its aeonic evolutionary path.

Much of this was yet to come, so that when Charles Fillmore took his strong stand for Christ in the first decade of this century, he was indeed a pioneer in this realm of unfolding thought. And most re-freshing of all was his "next step," his open statement that he was a personal disciple of Christ. Charles was indeed a herald trumpeting in full vigor.

In *Christian Healing* Charles quoted Jesus on nearly every page, declaring in effect: Here is the Man who proved what He said about divinity; let us obey His precepts. It seemed to Charles that whatever metaphysical system one might adopt, to leave Jesus out of the system was like leaving Moses out of the Pentateuch, or I AM THAT I AM out of the revelation on Mount Horeb.

And since Charles was not capable of half measures, he spoke and acted as if he were a personal disciple of Jesus in Kansas City. It is a step difficult to describe in this day, two thousand years after Jesus walked the hills of Galilee.

I tried to envision this step during an interview with May Rowland. We were speaking of Charles Fillmore and I said, "There are times when Charles Fillmore writes so intimately about Jesus that I get the impression he is writing almost as if he were a personal disciple of Jesus. Did he ever say anything to you along those lines?"

"Charles felt that he knew Jesus," May Rowland replied spontaneously. There was not a shadow of hesitation in her reply. "Charles felt that Jesus was his friend."

I kept silent for a few moments. We were in May Rowland's home, *Casa Serena*, seated in her living room. Its windows look out on a gentle sloping hillside, and for an instant I seemed to be gazing at the pleasant hills of Galilee. I looked into May Rowland's eyes and saw a vision there that could not be put into words—at least my words —so I kept quiet.

Presently May continued, "Charles always spoke of feeling the presence of the Christ."

I finally found my voice. "Did he ever speak of seeing Jesus?"

"He spoke of feeling Him. Again and again he would speak of Jesus as a real presence. He felt himself in intimate contact with Jesus. He made you actually feel the presence of the Christ. There were times," May Rowland continued, "that I almost felt like looking around to see if Jesus was in the room."

"May I quote you?" I asked.

"Of course. Charles would often say, 'I am a walking disciple of Christ.' Sometimes he would sign a letter with his name and add: 'Representative of Christ at Large.' "

"And this was always so?" I asked. "I mean, from the very beginning?"

"So far as I know, yes. I met Charles Fillmore about fifty years ago and at that time he was speaking of himself as 'a representative of Christ at large.' I should add, however, that as time went on he became more and more certain of his relationship."

"You mean certain of the friendship of Christ?"

"Yes. At the last he spoke more of Christ than of Jesus. But whether he spoke of Jesus as the man, or Christ as principle, he spoke from intimate knowledge and feeling."

This is the essential quality that gives the message of Charles Fillmore its note. There is an intimacy in the message which goes beyond the presentation of a mere reasonable belief. It is the difference between a theological dissertation on the vicarious atonement and the message of the disciple who knew Jesus intimately when he said, "That . . . which we have heard, which we have seen with our eyes, which we have looked upon, and our hands have handled, of the Word of Life . . . declare we unto you" (I John 1: 1-3).

Another idea presented in *Christian Healing* was so new at the time that it evoked little recognition. Even today the idea may seem reasonable from a cosmic point of view, but it receives little more than lip service and is beyond the teachings found in orthodox circles.

Charles wrote: "The perfect-man idea in God-Mind is known under various names in the many religious systems." Though this may receive some nods of approval today, the next sentence often does not: "The Krishna of the Hindu is the same as the Messiah of the Hebrews."

Swami Vivekananda in his lectures was saying much the same kind of thing at the same time, and those who heard him were impressed in accordance with their own degree of understanding.

The words of Vivekananda concerning Jesus are now well known: "Had I lived in Palestine in the days of Jesus of Nazareth I would have washed his feet, not with my tears but with my heart's blood."*

* *The Life of Swami Vivekananda* by his Eastern and Western disciples. Advaita Ashrama. Calcutta, 1965. p. 449.

12 Continuing Growth

Soon the growth of Unity as a movement and of the three magazines
—*Unity, Wee Wisdom,* and *Weekly Unity*—made larger quarters
necessary. The lot at 917 Tracy Avenue next door to number 913
was purchased, a larger building was erected, and the printing plant
was moved to the new quarters in September 1910.

Growth was taking place beyond the dreams of the Fillmores. That
was all to the good, but still income and outgo were equal. There was
no accumulation of funds.

Many people wished to purchase the magazines but could not
afford to do so though the nominal subscription prices were low:
Each of the three magazines cost only $1.00 a year. So Charles and
Myrtle organized Silent–70, a department through which free literature would be sent to those who asked for it. Subscribers were soon
writing in to ask that magazines be sent free to their friends. Indeed,
in one issue of *Unity*, the editors asked subscribers to be "sparing
in their requests." Charles wrote: "Our free list now costs over ten
dollars per week and is growing very fast."

Ten dollars a week meant a good deal to Unity. In those days men
got married on ten dollars a week. On Sunday mornings the total
offering at the Unity Society service often yielded less than ten dollars.

Yet Charles and Myrtle did not restrict their giving. Unity depended on what others gave—how was it possible for the founders of the movement not to give? Within a short time the need in public institutions came to their attention and magazines were also sent by Silent–70 to prisons, hospitals, libraries, and other institutions.

James Dillet Freeman says, "One time early in the history of Unity, a subscriber sent in one hundred dollars for a hundred-year subscription to Unity. It is hard to imagine the gratitude to God that the one hundred dollars evoked in the Unity office."

In the course of their lives Charles and Myrtle had to answer many questions about money. One of the most frequent questions, perhaps the inevitable one, was, "How is Unity supported?" Charles and Myrtle would often reply, "Through prayer."

Myrtle Fillmore's constant assertion was that the money flowing into Unity came from God. A former staff worker says that sometimes, when the staff was about to have a meeting, Myrtle would ask her, "Are you going to have a meeting about finances?"

"If I said 'yes,' Myrtle would reply, 'Then I will not be there.' " The friend adds, "Need I say that Myrtle did not simply absent herself? She preferred to take the matter up privately in prayer."

On one occasion, James Dillet Freeman says, when the headquarters staff knew that they had little money and that expenses were piling up, a worker said, "Let us pray that the money will hold out."

"Oh, no!" said Myrtle. "Let us pray that our faith will hold out."

In 1914 Charles merged his various departments—the Unity Tract Society (formerly the Unity Book Company), the Society of Silent Unity, the Unity Correspondence School, and Silent–70—into a single corporation: "The Unity School of Christianity." The term "school," Charles felt, described the fundamental work of the movement.

In spite of the new building at 917 Tracy Avenue, Unity headquarters soon needed even more space. So 913 Tracy Avenue was enlarged. A front section was added to the original building, which was moved to the back of the lot, and a fourth floor was added to the entire structure. On December 31, 1914, a New Year's Eve festival was held to celebrate the opening of this new Unity administration building.

Weekly Unity reported that four hundred people were served sandwiches, cakes, apples, cocoa, and cereal coffee. "At the stroke of twelve the darkened administration building suddenly flashed into light; the front door swung open and the chimes began to ring."

World War I touched the Fillmores intimately. Rickert Fillmore joined the armed forces. Economic stringencies limited the expansion of Unity. The cost of living increased, while the goodwill offerings at Sunday services still remained at a total of about ten dollars. Classes taught at Unity School yielded only small amounts. Myrtle Fillmore was keenly conscious of the needs of her associates at headquarters, and during this period, as well as before and after the war, she would often send her secretary into a class to "put something for the teacher into the collection plate," as James Dillet Freeman expresses it.

At other times when Myrtle knew that someone was in financial need, she would leave money on that worker's typewriter. Charles was likewise solicitous for the workers of Unity. An appeal for a job from anyone would always touch him in a tender spot. He would create a job, or ask Myrtle to do so, or appeal to a co-worker to find a convenient place for the needy person.

Dr. Marcus Bach tells one story of such an occasion: "There is a woman here who needs help," Charles said to a co-worker. "Give her a job."

"But we have no jobs to give!"

"Create a job for her," said Charles. She needs money in order to get her dental plates. She is toothless. Give her a job."

There was a "tower room" at 917 Tracy Avenue for night workers, and Charles and Myrtle often came to this room to join them for their nine o'clock prayer meeting. In front of the fireplace there was a rocking chair which Charles liked, and he would often sit there rocking in deep content. Sometimes he would sit in silence; at other times he would answer questions; on occasion before the night session began he would sing.

"How Charles loved to sing!" his friends all say. He liked Gilbert and Sullivan songs, and he sang, beating time to their rollicking rhythm and smiling with delight at their humor. *The Mikado* was his favorite operetta.

In 1919 Charles Fillmore was in his sixty-fifth year. He had been founder, publisher, editor, writer, counselor, lecturer, teacher, for over thirty years, working day after day, far into the night, snatching a few hours' sleep and guiding Unity with every waking thought. Even in his sleep his dreams were often concerned with his work for Unity's progress.

Biologists and psychologists often speak of the sixties as a climacteric period of life when certain physical and mental changes take place, sometimes producing a crisis. Charles Fillmore never for a moment accepted such chronological limitations, and he was put to the test in 1919. After thirty years of unremitting labor, he passed through a physical crisis. He did not waver for a moment, though his illness became severe. There were months when he had to hold fast to life, as he had done when he was a boy of eleven. He had fought the battle before, and he would fight it again.

Close friends knew his condition, and some of them confessed later that they wondered whether he would survive. But there was Silent Unity, and the prayers of that blessed group were his. There was Myrtle Fillmore, and her brave standing-by was a source of comfort to him. His three sons were also faithfully present. There were his friends, who would welcome him gladly at the office whenever he made his appearance. And there was the Christ.

And because it is not within the purview of Unity to give power to illness, or to fear its signs, Charles found prayerful support on every side. When he was unable to lecture for several months at the Sunday services, his friends stood by—not helplessly, but praying with him in faith.

Some of these early workers are today honored in Unity history: Cora Dedrick, secretary to Charles and Myrtle Fillmore; Mrs. Jennie H. Croft, librarian, teacher, healer; May Rowland; E. V. Ingraham; Richard Lynch.

In the end, affirming his divinity as he had taught others to do, Charles won his battle. What had he, the son of God, to do with climacterics? By the time the year 1920 dawned Charles Fillmore was stronger and his friends were rejoicing in his renewed vigor.

The Fillmores began to think of still larger headquarters, possibly away from the bustle and noise of Kansas City. Tracy Avenue downtown had become a busy industrial and commercial area. Perhaps they should consider some village or farm where all the workers could live in easy proximity to their work, where they could find time to relax and rest and pray.

Rickert Fillmore, home from service in the armed forces, liked the idea, and so did Lowell Fillmore. They began to cull newspaper advertisements of farms for sale, and one Sunday afternoon in February 1920 they drove out to a farm which had been advertised. Upon arrival they found that the place had just been sold. When the real-estate agent was told what they needed, he declared that he knew just the right farm and promptly took them to a farm of fifty-eight acres.

"Here you are," he said. "This is just what you need. It is a quiet place, not too far from the city, with the right amount of space."

Charles, Lowell, and Rickert all liked the place and Charles made one of his prompt decisions.

"We like it," he said. "And we'll take it!" They made a down payment, and Unity Farm came into being.

13 The Human Touch

The activities at Tracy Avenue kept on increasing. The popularity of Unity Inn as "that vegetarian place" with its excellent meals resulted in the erection in 1920 of a vegetarian cafeteria in a new building at the corner of Tracy Avenue and Ninth Street. The new Unity Inn was decorated by Rickert Fillmore and was known as the best vegetarian cafeteria in the United States. It served Unity workers and visitors from all over the city, as well as hundreds from out of town.

Eric Butterworth likes to tell a story about Charles and Myrtle Fillmore and their visits to Unity Inn.

"I was always much impressed," Eric Butterworth says, "to see Charles and Myrtle in line at mealtimes, like everybody else. They would take their place with their trays and proceed step by step, no matter how long the line, and sometimes it was very long. Unless you knew who they were you would never imagine that those two people were the founders of Unity."

And Eric always adds, "It was such a human thing, and so natural that you had to really think about it to realize that Charles and Myrtle were not being 'democratic,' as people say nowadays when executives meet with employees. These two were simply being the warm, friendly, unostentatious human beings that they were at heart. They were simply being themselves, and that was that." It became natural at about this time for Charles to be called affectionately "Papa Charles," and Myrtle, "Mama Myrtle."

Royal Fillmore saw the tremendous possibilities of radio as a medium long before other religious organizations turned to radio broadcasts. In 1922 he encouraged Francis J. Gable to broadcast Unity talks over station WOQ, Kansas City. Radio was still in its infancy and WOQ was the first broadcasting station to be licensed in the Middle West. Of course radio broadcasts aroused a great deal of interest, and inasmuch as Francis Gable broadcast his talks from the window of a downtown store, crowds gathered on the sidewalk to watch the sight.

In his thirty-fourth year Royal Fillmore, always robust, became ill. Everything possible was done for him, but after many weeks of illness he passed away on September 9, 1923. Royal was a warm, outgoing man of great promise. Charles and Myrtle had looked forward to his help, for he had shown talent in spreading the teachings of Unity among businessmen. In their quiet way his parents accepted the consolations of their friends, carrying on the work of Unity. Often they gave comfort to those who came to bring them comfort.

The world knows that Charles and Myrtle were proponents of spiritual healing, but does it realize that spiritual healers have their own Gethsemane? A question that every conscientious doctor asks when his patient dies is, Did I fail to see what should have been done? This question also challenges a spiritual healer in his realm.

The Fillmores knew that prayer heals every manner of disease; countless testimonies in the files of Silent Unity and cases that they knew of personally bore witness to the fact that prayers heal the disease to which Royal had succumbed. So there was a deeper problem. Why do certain cases come to this end? Could the answer be put into words? Soul progress? The necessity for spiritual evolution?

For Charles and Myrtle there was no death. They knew life to be eternal. Reincarnation was a fact: The one they knew as Royal was still going on his exuberant way, and they were sure that he would return again at the right time to fulfill his divine destiny.

In their own way on this solemn path Charles and Myrtle worked out their individual problems. Their answers were not identical—a fact which puzzled some followers in the early days, but which has proved to be a blessing to Unity students. For instead of promulgating a fixed point of view the Fillmores were able to give Truth students an open-ended view of death. In these days when ecclesiastical teachings regarding death offer little intelligent comfort, Unity students have a tranquil, well-balanced view of death, reasonable teachings regarding the afterlife, and a sanative attitude—all of which are rare in our time.

In their writings henceforth the Fillmores said much about reincarnation and death, inculcating in Unity students a wholesome and sane attitude toward these problems. It is an attitude which the world greatly needs, pre-empting despair, hopelessness, and ineradicable sorrow.

In the course of his teachings Charles henceforth reiterated his firm stand that for him death was to be conquered in this incarnation. A few years later, in *Unity*, August 1929, he was saying to his students, "Do not throw cold water on me when I say that I am doing my best to follow Jesus in overcoming the death of my body."

There is a certain poignancy in this plea, and an implicit hope that his followers would come to understand his vantage point.

Myrtle Fillmore would express her own beliefs in letters to her friends and in answers to questions during her class teachings. Her feelings are well expressed in the chapter, "Transition," in *Myrtle Fillmore's Healing Letters.* In one letter she wrote, "Your son would not have you clinging to him in thought; nor would he wish you to come to him through death. He is a splendid soul, and would have you learn the truth and live it here and now."

In another letter Myrtle said to a bereaved friend, speaking of death, "And so to her it is a rest, an opportunity, to lay aside the body for a time and to break the conscious connection with things going on around her, until the divine urge within her again prompts her to build the body temple and take lessons here in the physical."

Myrtle Fillmore reiterated her belief regarding death shortly before her passing. She declared that she had worked long enough at her task as co-founder of the movement, and that she was going to take a rest.

Although Charles Fillmore's personal attitude toward death was not the same as Myrtle's, there was no inherent contradiction between them regarding the function of death in the human scheme.

Many who have studied these matters agree that in the final stages of spiritual attainment, when the near-adept is about to complete his round of incarnations, he takes the viewpoint expressed by Charles. Other souls, also nearing the end of their experience on planet Earth, prefer to take periods of rest, which they not only welcome, but determine for themselves, as Myrtle Fillmore did. Both views are legitimate, being in accordance with soul-needs; and both aid students on their respective paths.

In the scheme of spiritual evolution there are others, like Royal, who might garner fruitage for soul-progress through a comparatively short incarnation. The ultimate demonstration of life everlasting, life with no recurrent cycles of death, is still the goal, still the aim ever before the vision of those who understood the message of the Christ. Such teachings, hammered out on the anvil of their own life experience by the Fillmores, have blessed Unity and have given Truth students a salutary attitude toward life and death.

In 1924, two years after Francis Gable began the Unity broadcasts, station WOQ was offered for sale. Broadcasts had become so popular that Unity purchased the station. The WOQ studio was moved to 917 Tracy Street. Radio fans in those days were proud of "getting distance," logging stations all over the country far into the night. From all quarters people wrote that they had "picked up" WOQ and liked the message.

Charles soon developed into a masterly radio broadcaster. Every week he gave two or three talks, and three or four times a month he would give a talk at 2:00 or 3:00 A.M. Since there were few radio stations in the Middle West, and still fewer with early morning programs, Charles found a wide audience. Some people sat up to hear Charles; others set their alarm clocks for the early morning hours and woke up to listen to him.

Workers at headquarters often saw Charles in the height of summer broadcasting with perspiration streaming down his face, his shirt wet from his exertions, but as keen as ever after an hour's broadcast. There were no cooling systems in those early days. The WOQ studio had electric fans, but since they introduced noise which the station picked up, they were turned off during broadcasts. It was hot work, but Charles enjoyed every moment of it.

Another important feature of Unity was the publication of *Daily Word* on July 1, 1924, edited by Frank B. Whitney. Just as there are some stories known within a family which add keen interest to certain events, so within the staff headquarters there are Unity stories which add a meaningful tone to certain circumstances. The story of Frank Whitney is a good example. He came to Unity headquarters after World War I in the hope of finding his lifework. He had high talent, but like many returning servicemen he found it difficult to settle down and to decide what he truly wanted.

Frank Whitney was outspoken, and something of a maverick; indeed, some of the headquarters staff were doubtful of his future in Unity.

"Leave him alone!" said Myrtle. "He'll find himself."

And Frank Whitney did indeed find himself. He became dean of the Unity Correspondence School. In 1924 he conceived the idea of *Daily Word* and launched the magazine with the Fillmores' happy approval. *Daily Word* is now the best known of all Unity publications. It is accepted as nondenominational by many denominations —there can be no higher praise.

Charles Fillmore's interest in his young helpers is also remembered with gratitude by many workers today at Unity Village. Ralph Rhea, Coordinator, Unity School, said to me, "If it were not for Papa Charles, I would not be here in Unity now. He saved me when I might have been dismissed, or at least eased out somehow."

"Are you sure of that?" I asked. "Unity people seem so warm and friendly . . ."

"I'll tell you the story," said Ralph, "and you can judge for yourself. I was a boy at the time, and I was full of mischief. We had a very hot summer that year in Kansas City, and added to the heat was a severe drought. As you know, Unity believes that the weather can be controlled, or to put it another way, Unity believes that the weather is under God's jurisdiction. So there were daily prayers for rain. Once the Silent Unity workers were gathered together on the top floor at Tracy Avenue, praying for rain.

"I was up on the roof and I could just hear their voices. Near me on the roof was a tub with water in it, and a sudden impulse seized me. While they were praying I caught hold of the tub and tipped it to let water pour down the side of the building in a slow stream. I remember thinking, 'Let them have their rain!' Of course I was a young boy, and I did it in a wild moment.

"You can imagine the result! Some of the older heads were sure I wasn't the right person for Unity after that!

"But Papa Charles laughed! He did not get angry, and he said to them, 'Leave the boy alone, he is good material. He'll find himself.'

"So here I am now," Ralph Rhea said. "And when you ask me how I remember Papa Charles, this is the first memory that emerges. It is an event that represents, for me, the essence of the man."

Before I could make any comment Ralph Rhea said, "And I have other memories of Papa Charles. They are more intimate because they have more to do with him as a counselor. He helped me many times, so I can speak from experience.

"I've said I was a little wild at times—pouring water down from the roof is just an example. But in spite of that I was filled with fears.

I did not grow up in an easy time. There was World War I, you know, and then there was the Great Depression, and other things.

"Papa Charles gave me a feeling of assurance when I talked to him. He always spoke quietly when he was counseling, and somehow one always felt that he was also speaking prayerfully. One got a feeling from him that it was possible to meet any situation and come through unhurt.

"Once when I confessed to a great fear Papa Charles said, 'You like to ride horses, don't you?'

" 'Yes,' I replied.

" 'Well, treat your fear as if it were a horse. When you are riding a horse if it bucks at a piece of paper you pull it up short. You speak to the horse, don't you? You say to it, "Now don't be afraid! That's only a piece of paper!" And you take the horse past the piece of paper. Perhaps you say to the horse, "That's only a piece of paper! It can't do you any harm!" '

"Of course, I could understand that, and I could appreciate the illustration. And I said so.

" 'Well,' Papa Charles continued, 'when a fear occurs, treat it like that piece of paper! Ride the emotion—take control. Say, "That's only a piece of paper. It can't harm me!" And ride past the emotion with a firm hand on the reins.' "

Ralph Rhea smiled. "And that bit of advice has helped me all my life. That is how Papa Charles taught. He always spoke simply, and he was always full of helpful illustrations and humorous sidelights. He never delivered an oration. He spoke to you. It was a heart-to-heart conversation. For me that has always been proof of his genius as a teacher."

14 The Forty-Year Fruitage

When President Coolidge was re-elected in 1924, having become president through the death of President Harding, the national slogan was normalcy. To this was added another cry: prosperity. Higher prices on the stock market, and a free flow of money—these "proofs" of normalcy and affluence pleased the nation. The workers at Unity Village who remember those days say that for the first time the headquarters payroll at Tracy Avenue could be met with some facility. There had been occasions when salaries at headquarters were postponed for a few days, sometimes even for a week. The staff was always paid in the end, but their mode of life involved sacrifices of which no one spoke.

I once heard a businessman on the plaza of Unity Village eulogizing the architecture, the well-maintained buildings, the offices, the fountain, the gardens. He was with two members of the administrative staff, who had stopped to speak to him near the fountain.

"It must be wonderful to work in such an atmosphere," he said. "And for a prosperous organization too! You are lucky!"

They smiled, and I accompanied them to the administrative building. After the executive member of the staff entered his office, his assistant remarked, "That man had no idea he was speaking to someone whose salary had been postponed several times in the old days because we had no money in the till. Nor does he know that in those days the salary was barely sufficient for food and shelter. We wore the same suits for years!"

Tracy Avenue was a bustling center in the late 1920s, and the entire plant was overcrowded. Three buildings had been erected within the interior of the property. The broadcasting studio was in a building unit which housed the heating plant and the repair shops. After living on Elmwood Avenue for several years, Charles and Myrtle had moved to the upper floors of the broadcasting studio. Here they had an apartment which looked out on what Myrtle spoke of facetiously as "Gasoline Alley."

Rickert was determined to put an end to Gasoline Alley for his parents, and in 1925 he built one of the first cottages at Unity Farm for them. Here, seventeen miles outside of Kansas City, Charles and Myrtle could have a comfortable home in the pleasant, rolling countryside.

Five years had passed since Unity Farm was purchased. Building activities on the farm were slow because there were no surplus funds and transforming the farm into Unity headquarters required a goodly outlay.

The home built for Charles and Myrtle was called "The Arches." It was a Cotswold cottage, but the rooms were surprisingly spacious. The Cotswold cottages in England had charmed Rickert when he was there as a soldier in World War I, so he chose their architectural style and room arrangement for the farm. He placed the cottage in the middle of an apple orchard, and built it with arches, a peaked roof, gables, casement windows, and nooks. It was Myrtle's "dream house," for Rickert had planned it with his mother.

In a literal sense it was also what Myrtle called her fairy home, for it had no kitchen.

"No kitchen!" Charles exclaimed when he first heard of the scheme. "Not even a hot plate?"

"Not while we have Grandma across the road," replied Myrtle.

"Cooking is her joy. All we have to do is to walk across the road. Don't you think we've done our share of entertaining in the past?"

Charles' fondness for entertaining was often a source of family amusement. Charles was so outgoing and genial that he habitually invited people home for dinner on the slightest excuse.

And Grandma Fillmore happily cooked at all times for unexpected guests. At the same time Myrtle felt a duty toward her guests and never withdrew from them. So she was always a busy, welcoming hostess. In her dream house Myrtle wanted to invite her soul and not spend time as a busy hostess. Charles acquiesced.

Myrtle was most solicitous about Grandma, however, and now that they could manage it she saw that Grandma had help in the kitchen. In fact in the latter days it is said that Grandma became the Queen Victoria of her kitchen and supervised the cooking with all the aplomb of Victoria at her court.

There was a gracious relationship between Myrtle and Grandma Fillmore. They were both strong characters, yet each in her respective realm blessed the other and expressed the warmth of family love. They were both happy persons.

When Grandma was in her late nineties she fell and broke her hip. Myrtle promised her a wheelchair but Grandma replied, "A wheelchair for me? I am no invalid! Thank you, my dear, but I'll use my rocking chair!"

So with the aid of Charles and some of the carpenters on the farm the rocking chair was transformed into a kind of sled on wheels.

"It is really a rocking chair with rollers," Myrtle declared, "like the rollers on skates. My, how Grandmother does ride around on it! She motors all over the house, and she's the engine, the gas, the chauffeur, and the backseat driver all in one."

But Charles and Myrtle did not move out completely from Tracy Avenue to live at The Arches. So far as they were concerned it would be a country house until Tracy Avenue was moved to the farm. On Sundays they conducted the Tracy Avenue service as usual, left in the afternoon for the farm, and returned to Tracy Avenue on Monday morning. There they remained, doing administrative work, counseling, working with Silent Unity, and conducting the Wednesday evening healing meetings. On Thursdays they left again for the farm to spend the evening at The Arches. On Friday morning they would be back at their Gasoline Alley apartment on Tracy Avenue, remaining until Sunday for the chapel service.

There was only a dirt road leading to the farm in those early days. Today a broad concrete highway—State Highway 50—runs past the entrance to Unity Village.

By 1925 the annual conference of Unity teachers had become a sizable group. As always, there was great freedom of opinion, but some of the teachers felt that a certain unanimity of thought was needed. At their summer meeting they adopted a set of rules, outlined a code of conduct for Unity teachers, and established the "Unity Annual Conference."

When the teachers told Charles about their action, his answer was characteristic: "I can't see why you want to bind yourselves with a lot of rules and regulations. Leave yourselves free!" Characteristic also was his remark when he later saw the wisdom of the move: "I can see that the step you took was a necessary one."

The Unity teachers finally formed a strong organization called the "Unity Ministers' Association." For many years this association carried on its activities, governing the teaching and conduct of the centers and churches in cooperation with Unity School. At length the Unity School administration decided to divest itself of such control, and the association became the "Association of Unity Churches," an independent corporate entity. Today this self-governing body sets the standards for some two hundred Unity churches, centers, associations, and fellowships in the United States and throughout the world.

Charles Fillmore's second book, *Talks on Truth,* appeared in

1926, seventeen years after his first, *Christian Healing*. To those unfamiliar with the story of Charles Fillmore, the span of time between both books belies the fact that he was one of the most prolific writers and teachers of his time. His editorials and magazine articles, notes for the Wednesday healing services and Sunday morning services, notes for classes in practical Christianity, meetings given over to questions and answers, all constituted a work load of writing and teaching which few teachers nowadays would carry.

Talks on Truth was based on notes which Charles enlarged and elaborated to form a synthesis of his most important teachings. It was a progressive presentation—the next step after his *Christian Healing*. His own advancing grasp of the Christ-principle and of the techniques for practical spiritual development made the book a necessity. It is the book of a pioneer of thought, with topics covering an extraordinary range of ideas.

The pioneer of thought who expresses a new idea opens up the way for its exploration by other thinkers. Further elaboration and courageous exploration of new meanings ultimately bring the idea within the realm of popular acceptance. Without the pioneer, moreover, there would be little progress in the realm of ideas. Conventional thinking, orthodox reasoning, placid acceptance—these blaze no path of progress. In the end the idea which has enriched us seems to be our normal heritage, but this is a fallacy. Original thinkers have been derided, denounced, sometimes crucified, and thus clarity of thought demands that we recognize such courage. As warriors honor their heroes, so should thinkers honor pioneers of thought.

The pioneer in the realm of metaphysical truth and its practical application necessarily lifts his followers above the common round of ideas. Charles Fillmore, for instance, presented ideas regarding the body far above the accepted opinions of his time. In *Talks of Truth* he formulated techniques, drills, and practices which enabled students to maintain health and to practice spiritual healing for themselves and others.

This is one of the chief virtues of metaphysical thought and of the modern metaphysical movement. It gives students a point of view which enables them to rise above the norm; and there is no student of human affairs who does not admit that the norm of ordinary human life is low. In fact our norm today is a sub-norm. As a result the man in the street can benefit from metaphysical presentations of truth and gain a standard of health, happiness, and wholeness far ahead of our hapless conventional norm.

Thus ideas regarding the body, as presented in *Talks on Truth,* were far ahead of their time. Even today, nearly fifty years later, what Charles says about the human body seems visionary to some people, but modern science is presenting a view regarding the body which points in the direction of Charles' vision. The word psychosomatic had not yet become popular when his book was written, but much that Charles Fillmore said about the potent influence of the mind on the body is accepted today by psychologists and biologists. His view still goes beyond modern psychomatic theories because it embraces the effect of spiritual understanding on our mental and physical processes.

The important point is that students who accepted his view used techniques and ideas which benefited them and lifted them above the norm of their day.

What Charles said about microbes and microorganisms was both startling and radical. He declared that the germ is not the ultimate factor in causing disease; this was indeed a unique statement. The hypothesis that there is another factor in the cause of disease is beginning to make sense today, but in the first part of this century it seemed nonsense. The masses of the western world had imbibed the fear of germs with their mother's milk. Pasteur had done his great work in the 1880s, and the generation which grew under the impact of his theories had raised another generation of children even more firmly committed to the germ theory.

Yet Charles Fillmore said of microbes: "They are not responsible for their existence; they are formed vehicles of thought, and are the servants of those who gave them life. . . . All counterfeit thought comes from the intellect, which alone originates the disease germ and the destructive microbe. Appearances say that microbes are dangerous and destructive, but one who is familiar with their origin is not alarmed, because he knows that there is a power and wisdom stronger and wiser than the ignorant intellect."

Other statements in *Talks on Truth* regarding the body are basic for students who wish to understand spiritual healing. "The true body," said Charles, "is an ethereal body." He also spoke of vibrant centers of consciousness within the body—a development which he brought to its height in another book four years later, *The Twelve Powers of Man.*

Charles Fillmore's books, when studied chronologically, take on a profound significance as progressive presentations of an unfolding science of being. The steps of his unfolding revelation can be seen, and the orderly unfoldment of his ideas can be recognized. In this way a student can grasp his comprehensive vision with comparative ease.

Once again Charles spoke as the universal man, quoting the Buddha in exquisite words translated thus by Sir Edwin Arnold in *The Light of Asia:*

> The soul of things is sweet,
> The Heart of Being is celestial rest;
> Stronger than woe is will;
> That which was Good doth pass to better, best.

The vision which enabled Charles to discover the essence of truth in the religions of the world is nowhere better exemplified than in this quotation, which goes directly to the heart of the Buddha's teaching.

Charles made a short trip to New York in 1926, where he was well received, speaking to crowds in a simple manner that astonished many New Yorkers. They were looking for an orator, perhaps an evangelist. He spoke directly to them like a friend.

A Unity counselor who remembers Charles' visit to New York says, "Several times I saw him step down from the platform after his talk and choose someone out of the group pressing forward to speak to him. Then he would lead that person to a convenient chair in the auditorium. After a few words Charles would close his eyes and go into the silence and pray right there, oblivious of all the commotion around. That taught me a lot about counseling, and about meeting the need immediately, wherever and whenever I see it."

The changing pattern of Kansas City was transforming Tracy Avenue into an industrial district, so in 1928 the Unity Society of Practical Christianity purchased a lot on the outskirts of town for a new Unity temple. The location was on 47th and Jefferson Streets, and Charles marked a fieldstone on the lot after it was purchased, saying, "One day a mighty temple will rise here for the Unity Society of Practical Christianity."

The prophecy was fulfilled when the Unity Temple was dedicated at that location twenty-two years later, in 1950. In the meantime, this area in Kansas City had become famous as Country Club Plaza, one of the best-planned developments of its time.

Charles felt that the time had also come for Unity headquarters to move to the farm. Of course he was by no means alone in this decision. Myrtle, Lowell, and Rickert were eager for the move. In those days Rickert's time was taken up wholly in planning for the change and in starting construction at the farm.

Transforming the farm into headquarters for Unity was no simple matter. Water, for instance, presented a problem. Drilling for wells had not proved successful, so Rickert decided to build a large lake capable of supplying the entire community.

Rickert built his lake, flooding twenty-two acres of land. At the concrete dam there was a drop of fifty feet. When it was finished in 1927 it was the largest artificial lake in Jackson County.

The next problem was the building of a water tower which would be large enough to supply all the requirements of the community. Rickert did not build an industrial water tank; he built a tower of architectural grace and beauty—Unity Tower, now a landmark in Jackson County and a familiar symbol to Unity students throughout the United States and the world.

As noted earlier, the Tower is one hundred and sixty-five feet high. When completed, it contained seven stories of offices, including the tank with a total capacity of one hundred thousand gallons of water.

First to be erected was the Silent Unity building. There was symbolic importance in the decision to erect this building first. "In the beginning is the Word"—the word of prayer, this act declared. "Let the heart beat first," the new office building affirmed, for the heart of Unity is prayer—Silent Unity.

Work at Unity Farm then began in earnest. Rickert Fillmore with his architectural talent would mirror Charles' vision in a beautiful group of buildings, creating a garden village. Lowell Fillmore with his executive talent would foster that vision and "manage the works." Myrtle Fillmore, wife, mother, co-founder of Unity, would add her faith and the work of her hands and spirit.

Rickert and Lowell were in their forties, and their sympathy and understanding blessed the lives of Charles and Myrtle with fullness and warmth. It was a time of fruitage and joy for the entire family.

In 1928 Charles acquired his first automobile, a Ford. It became the family car at once, and one of the young workers at Tracy Avenue was always glad to drive Charles and Myrtle to the farm.

The year 1928 was of historic importance. That summer Unity leaders from all over the United States and abroad converged on the farm for a colossal tent convention. Unity Farm became a tent city, with over a hundred tents sheltering more than three hundred people. Sheltering is the right word, for it rained and rained and rained and rained. For the eight days of the convention Unity students sloshed through the rain with good humor and grateful hearts.

Apart from the Tower, the Silent Unity office was the only new structure on the farm. It was by no means complete, but every foot of space was used. The chapel-to-be was converted into a cafeteria which served fifteen hundred meals daily for visitors to the convention. Shower baths and other toilet facilities were also set up in the building.

Through this happy convocation moved Charles and Myrtle, lining up for meals in the cafeteria, taking part in the meetings, joining in the prayers, greeting old friends and making new ones who would remember that summer all their lives. They would remember Charles and Myrtle as quiet, friendly folk. They would remember Charles Fillmore's outgoing smile, his bright blue eyes, his keen sense of humor. They would remember Myrtle's gentle smile and gaze. They would remember the warmth of friendship that enveloped the whole gathering.

The workers from Tracy Avenue came in a body to the farm for one meeting—four hundred strong, forming a procession and singing hymns as they marched past the headquarters staff.

The Silent Unity building was dedicated on the last Sunday of the conference. More than two thousand people attended, and with the closing prayers Unity Farm was blessed, the Silent Unity building dedicated.

That was a memorable Sunday afternoon for the Fillmores. At the outdoor service Lowell and Rickert, with their wives, stood by Charles and Myrtle, while around them the larger Unity family of two thousand prayed. Forty years had passed since Myrtle and Charles had emerged from their darkness of pain and sorrow. Moses had seen the burning bush after forty years on Mount Horeb. For the Fillmores it was a day of spiritual joy, symbolically aflame with the promise of things to come.

Nearly a year later, on a beautiful spring day in 1929, the Silent Unity staff moved to their new building at Unity Farm. New telephones, new desks, a new office for Charles with a kitchen attached, a new office for Myrtle (no kitchen), a new chapel—a new order had begun.

15 "The Bond that Will Endure"

Spring at Unity Farm in 1929; spring in Jackson County in 1929; spring in the United States in 1929; spring and a financial boom; and then fall—October 1929, and the stock market crash. Within two years stock losses totaled fifty billion dollars.

The Great Depression is now history, never to be forgotten. Construction throughout the United States ceased, including that at Unity Farm. Early in 1930 Silent Unity left its new building at Unity Farm and returned to the old quarters at Tracy Avenue.

During the depression years the Unity Training School used the Silent Unity building for its ministerial students. The farm became a retreat where applicants could pursue their studies in the quiet of the countryside.

Charles Fillmore knew all about booms and busts. He had survived them before, and had proved superior to them. Was not Unity built on faith? In the hearts of Charles and Myrtle and the headquarters staff, and indeed of all earnest Unity students, faith burned like a flame. It was not a flame that could flare up for a time and then die down, perhaps to flare up once more and die down again; it was a faith that burned without ceasing.

Unity's survival might have seemed in the balance at the time, for Unity had no capital. I once put this problem up to a banker, stating the historical facts, but not mentioning the name Unity.

"Well," said the banker, "survival would be highly problematical, unless some unknown factor entered to save the movement."

What saved Unity was not an unknown factor, but the love factor. Unity had been built on love-offerings and happily the love-offerings from thousands of devoted followers kept Unity alive. The capital of many firms during the depression dwindled to nothing. Love did not dwindle: It proved to be the best capital.

Charles Fillmore's third book, *The Twelve Powers of Man*, was published in 1930. Once again the presentation was progressive, an expansion of his former teachings, a logical development of techniques. It bears repeating to emphasize that a student who tries to begin his studies with this book may have a difficult time without the necessary preparation. It is a book for practitioners of truth. It is a book of Christian yoga, for Christian yogins.

In one comprehensive sweep it coordinates metaphysical Truth in such a form that the book provides meditation, mantrams or affirmations, drills, and techniques for students who wish to embody their vision. In this respect it is a form of the eternal yoga. The various forms of yoga are useful for students of various types, but the essence of the matter is that yoga considers religious truths to be scientific facts that must be put into practice. A man must practice yoga to be a yogin. A philosopher is not a yogin; an intellectual is not a yogin; an artist is not a yogin. A yogin is one who practices yoga—not one who reads about it, or even studies it.

In this sense Jesus was a supreme teacher of yoga. The "yoke" of Jesus is a yoga. All of us know that Jesus said, "Take my yoke upon you . . ." and that he also declared, "For my yoke is easy, and my burden is light."

Instead of speaking of etheric centers and depicting them in the manner of books on yoga, Charles spoke of the body-centers as expressions of states of consciousness. He identified those states of consciousness with qualities of divine Mind. Each of the apostles typified a state of mind, Charles maintained, and he gave the centers names corresponding to the apostles, or states of consciousness.

Characteristically, in accordance with his vision, Charles gave the central control of all states of consciousness to Christ. As in yoga teachings, he placed the throne of this power in the top of the head.

The Twelve Powers of Man demands profound study and skilled practice on the part of the student. It may be a book of the future, for the future, but the ideas enunciated are profound and even startling. Charles said in his introduction, "It is not expected that beginners in the study of metaphysical Christianity will understand this book."

Charles also makes it clear that he presents what he has proved through practice. Some students have tried to discover whether he "borrowed" his presentation from yoga, or Rosicrucianism, or some other system. His own words may be accepted. In his *Talks on Truth* he had made it clear that he discovered these ideas himself by exploring his own consciousness, by examining his body mentally, and by turning to the Christ-principle within.

Sometimes in summer Charles and Myrtle gave classes at the Unity Training School on the farm. The school met in the chapel vacated by Silent Unity when depression had stopped the transfer of headquarters.

At one of their evening classes there occurred an incident which Unity students delight in recalling. The chapel was crowded, and everyone was enthusiastic, Charles supremely so. As Charles concluded his talk, he said to the crowd, "When this program is over, you are all invited to come over to our place for a bite to eat."

Myrtle rose to her feet and came forward.

"If you do," she said with a slight smile, "there had better be another expression of the miracle of the loaves and fishes."

Everyone at the farm knew about Myrtle's dream house without a kitchen, and the laughter that followed is a part of Unity's family history.

In all that he taught Charles Fillmore stressed the importance of principles. Those who had the privilege of his teaching speak again and again of his genius as a teacher in making them go back to fundamentals—to God as the Source of all, to Truth as the basis of thinking, to Christ as the exemplification of Truth.

Vera Dawson Tait spoke to me of the influence of one of Charles' favorite maxims on her life: " 'Always look for the thread that will lead you back to Truth,' Charles often declared. 'Whenever you find diverse opinions and conflicting theories, look for the thread that will lead you to the truth. If doubts ever assail you, look for the thread that will lead you back to Christ. You can find it.' "

Vera smiled when I asked her about Charles Fillmore and his teachings about Jesus.

"He would often say to us, 'We belong to Jesus,' " she replied. "For him this 'belonging' was an intimate relationship."

"You mean a personal relationship?"

"Yes. It was a direct relationship. And he kept on telling us we should have that direct relationship ourselves. You will find that direct relationship explained in many beautiful passages in *Teach Us to Pray.*"

Vera quoted freely. "We should talk directly to God instead of talking about Him. For instance, we are apt to say, 'God strengthens both my soul and my body.' Charles Fillmore always emphasized a more immediate relationship. He advised us to declare, 'Thy Spirit strengthens my soul,' instead of saying, 'God strengthens my soul.' You will find that"—Vera reached for the copy of *Teach Us to Pray* on her desk and flipped the pages—"on page 83."

"It seems to me," I said, "that you know that book by heart."

"Not quite," said Vera with a smile. She turned to the next page. " 'Jesus has fully bridged the gulf of separation. . . .' Charles says." She closed the book and continued, "That explains why he emphasized Jesus. He insisted that Jesus built this bridge to perfection for us and that it was sensible for us to use it."

Another friend of Charles Fillmore, L. E. Meyer, also told me of Charles' teachings with the knowledge of one who was an associate for over twenty years.

"Mr. Fillmore's emphasis on Jesus made a great impression on me from my very first day at Unity," he said. "Mr. Fillmore declared that since Jesus knew God intimately, and taught us to know God intimately, it was sensible to follow Him. But he went further. He maintained that an intimate relationship also exists between Jesus and His true followers, here and now—not in some other world— but here and now in this century."

"That alone would make him an unusual teacher," I remarked.

"More than that," added the Reverend Mr. Meyer. "There was an element of greatness in his teaching. You see, Mr. Fillmore would not only make beautiful statements about God, but he would teach us how to use them."

"Do you mean through drills, or practices?"

"You might call them that. For instance, Mr. Fillmore taught us to use the name Jesus with meaning. I remember once, when I was in need of physical healing, I called on the name of Jesus Christ continuously over a period of months. I must have called on the name of Jesus Christ ten thousand times or more."

"And you were healed?" It was needless to ask the question, for L. E. Meyer was in radiant health.

"Yes. You see, when one is in dire straits, as I was, it may not be easy to organize one's thoughts. Calling on the Name then becomes a supreme aid. Of course, Mr. Fillmore always said that in using the name Jesus we should do it with meaning, with an understanding of His love, wisdom, and power. It continues to be my practice today. It brings healing, and illumination, and peace."

It was good to hear these words from the man who was chaplain of Unity School.

"As chaplain your life here at Unity Village must be very rewarding," I remarked. "When did you first come to Unity?"

"In 1927. I was a chiropractor, a graduate of the Palmer School in Davenport, Iowa, but I had a physical condition which could not be healed. In desperation I turned to Unity teachings. I saw a counselor, asked for prayer, and that night I had my first rest in months. So I came to Kansas City and met Charles Fillmore. I wanted to know more about Unity, and it seemed a miracle to me that I could learn and work at the same time."

"Many of the ministerial students here at Unity Village feel the same way today," I remarked. "It is one of the great achievements of Charles Fillmore that he founded a school which enables some of its ministerial students to study and to pay their way at the same time by working. Was it so from the beginning?"

"Yes, from the beginning. And remember this was toward the end of the last century. In those days seminaries were endowed, or were supported by their church hierarchies. Charles Fillmore had no endowments, and there was no church hierarchy to support him."

"Subsequently you became a minister?" I asked.

"Yes. My ministerial service is a joy, but I must add that the five years I spent with Silent Unity was a special blessing as well as a joy."

"Is the training rigorous?" I asked.

"I would call it thorough—most thorough. Graduating from the ministerial class was just the beginning for me. The prayer work of Silent Unity not only requires a certain kind of dedication but also a certain degree of discipline and knowledge. I was put to work on the letters asking for prayer, and that was an education in itself. Answering each letter so as to meet the right need is a spiritual art. At first I was guided carefully, and my letters were sometimes corrected. But what finally impressed me most was Mr. Fillmore's confidence in me. There came a time when he said, 'Now you can answer these letters yourself through prayer. Try it—you can do it.' You see why I think he was a great teacher."

"When you say 'answer the letters through prayer,' do you mean that the worker who answers the letter also prays for the person who wrote the letter?"

"Yes. Of course you know that the names of the writers and their specific requests are also taken into the silent room for prayer by another specially trained worker," L. E. Meyer replied.

"Did you go through all these phases of prayer work in Silent Unity?" I asked.

"Yes, I worked in the letter department. I also worked in the prayer room itself—you know that the worker who enters this room stays there alone in prayer for half an hour."

"May I ask you a sharp question?" I ventured. "How do you work with the ministers of other religions?"

"Quite happily," L. E. Meyer replied. "Mr. Fillmore taught us to stress our likenesses with other religions rather than differences."

"Did he not say some rather strong things about religion at one time?" I asked.

"Yes, when he spoke about rigidity of dogma, or about literal interpretations of scripture, or about tyrannical authority. In religion he was against the same kind of thing that Jesus Christ was against. But he never spoke against the religious spirit, or the yearning in the human heart for religion. Of course you know that Unity is for the unity of all religions!"

Perhaps no teaching of Charles Fillmore has caused more comment than his acceptance of reincarnation. In the 1890s, when he spoke out so boldly about reincarnation, his words were startling. Sensible people knew that a man lived only once and that when he died he went to hell, purgatory, or heaven.

Charles Fillmore, however, never laid undue emphasis on reincarnation. He simply accepted it as a fact because he remembered past incarnations. Then he went on to teach his students that the acceptance of Jesus Christ's teachings would ultimately free them from the round of incarnations.

L. E. Meyer said, "The first time I heard Charles Fillmore speak he made a reference to reincarnation that was so casual I did not recognize it. He said, 'We have all been together before, and we will be together again.' I thought he was saying that some of the people in the class had attended former lectures and that we would all be listening to him again. Later I found out what he meant. To quote him again, 'We are kindred souls. In our search for God and His Truth we have as persons lived in this world before and been associated, and will after this life span be together again.' "

I asked May Rowland about Charles Fillmore's teachings along these lines, and she quoted Charles in much the same words. She made an addition which was even more interesting. "Once or twice Charles intimated that it would not be surprising if some of us had lived at the time of Jesus and had seen Him when He was in Palestine."

After a few moments of silence I ventured a remark. (When May Rowland says something important, she does not continue to talk. She lets the statement sink in.) "I suppose that means you are repeating—"

"Not repeating," May broke in. "Charles said the only reason for reincarnation was to go on to higher accomplishments."

Still interested in this view, I spoke to Vera Dawson Tait about it.

"Yes," Vera replied. "Charles said we had been together before and would be together again. For him it was simply a fact. Certainly there was a spiritual bond of friendship between all of us."

When I broached the matter to Ernest C. Wilson, he agreed wholeheartedly with the others and related a story that had profound inner meanings.

"Once," he said, "when I entered Mr. Fillmore's office with Frank Whitney, it became evident that we had interrupted a conversation. What this conversation was I do not know, though Mr. Fillmore's remark led me to believe it had something to do with Catholic priests who had given up the church. At any rate just as we walked into the office Charles Fillmore declared, 'Here comes another couple of Catholic priests now!' "

Ernest Wilson's face lighted up with a smile. "Mr. Fillmore, you know, had a delicate sense of humor. He felt that I had been in the priesthood before, and I suppose he thought the same thing about Frank Whitney. Certainly, he felt that some of us had been priests or nuns in the past. As for the man to whom he made the remark, I can still remember the surprise on his face."

All of Charles' friends say that he often spoke of Paul, so I asked Ernest Wilson, "How did Mr. Fillmore feel about Paul? I understand that he was very fond of him."

"I would say that Charles thought of himself at times as a kind of Paul."

"The thorn in the flesh?" I ventured.

"That, and other things," Ernest Wilson replied. "Paul broke away from the establishment, and so did Charles. As you know, there are some who say it was Paul who started the early church. Well, Charles Fillmore started Unity."

"Because you knew Charles Fillmore so well, may I ask you how you would characterize him? In describing Charles Fillmore I can say that he was of medium height, that his blue eyes often shone with humor, and that he was warm and friendly, but how can I describe his inner quality?"

Ernest Wilson pondered for a moment. "We were speaking of Paul," he said. "Mr. Fillmore had that inner quality of courage and conviction, that fiery, spiritual will so characteristic of Paul. He bowed to no difficulties. His own authority was his knowledge of Christ, like Paul's. But there is another man he reminds me of: Abraham Lincoln. Lincoln was tall and serious of mien. Charles was not tall, or serious, but he loved the people. His was the common touch. He was folksy. He had a keen sense of humor, enjoyed funny stories. Yes, I would say Charles was Lincolnesque in mind and heart."

Once again I returned to Charles Fillmore's love for Jesus. I had heard much of this from his other friends, but Ernest Wilson had been very close to Charles and had been chosen by him as the minister for the Unity Society of Practical Christianity in Kansas City. To my question about the relationship between Charles and Jesus, Ernest Wilson replied, "I can give you a good example of how Charles taught and felt in the way he always opened the Unity Conference of Ministers. It is an important annual conference, to which all the Unity ministers and teachers come. Charles always opened the conference with these words: 'This is the school of Jesus Christ.' "

"Did he use the same words for his other classes and courses?"

"Very often. Sometimes he would begin by saying, 'Jesus Christ is the head of this school.' When speaking to the Silent Unity workers he would say, 'Jesus Christ is the head of Silent Unity.' Perhaps I should add—and this is purely my own observation—that Charles spoke more of Christ than of Jesus in his later years.

"I shall always remember another remark of Mr. Fillmore's," Ernest Wilson continued. "Once a student of his intensive course spoke of leaving and Charles said, 'Do whatever you wish, go wherever you wish, *but do not leave out the name Christ.*' "

Lowell and Rickert had their own homes on the farm (paying rent in accordance with rules which still prevail in Unity Village), and Myrtle enjoyed visiting her family. Lowell Fillmore had married Alice Lee in 1926 and their house was close by. Rickert Fillmore had married Harriet Collins in 1919 and they had two children—Charles Rickert and Rosemary. They also lived in a house near The Arches, so that visits were easy. Myrtle especially enjoyed baby-sitting with her grandchildren.

In 1928 Charles Rickert was seven, Rosemary three years old. The children were always inviting Myrtle to play with them, though little invitation was needed. In the company of her grandchildren Myrtle, then in her eighties, became a child again. She described her life at this time in a letter to her sister: "You'd smile to see me rushing around, trying to keep up with the many things I find myself 'in for.' First, I want to look after some little thing at home; then meetings;

then the letters in the office; then another meeting or two; then a trip downtown; then a nap (if I can crowd one in); then an evening out; then a trip to the farm, and sometimes the care of one of the little folks; then the trip back, to take up work where I left off! And I just keep getting stronger, and younger, and happier, and more interested in things than ever."*

On March 29, 1931, Charles and Myrtle celebrated their fiftieth wedding anniversary. A simple but moving ceremony took place in the crowded chapel at 913 Tracy Avenue, where Ernest C. Wilson read the words of the Unity marriage rite.

"It was a touching event," Ernest Wilson declares, "and I had the impression that Myrtle took part in it with deeper feeling than we ourselves realized."

"What made you think so?" I asked.

"Well, I have thought a great deal about it. You see, later that year Myrtle began to remark to a few of her dearest friends that the time had come for her to depart."

"Did she say this to you herself?"

"Yes. There had been a few times, in earlier years, when Myrtle had spoken lightly of her passing. She had said to her friends that she felt she had accomplished as much as she could in this lifetime, and that the time would presently come for her to pass on. Sometimes she said that she wanted to leave, but it had been revealed to her that the time had not yet come. Now she felt that the time had come and she would soon depart."

Ernest Wilson continued, "I tried to dissuade Myrtle when she spoke of leaving us and she said, 'You know better than that, Ernest. You know there is no death. I have been doing this work for forty-five years. I have done all I can, and now I am tired. I can help more on the other side.' "

In his book *Household of Faith* Jim Freeman tells of a conversation

*James Dillet Freeman, *The Household of Faith*.

Myrtle had with a Unity worker a short time before her passing.

Myrtle liked to "visit with" the workers. They always welcomed her visits, feeling that her friendship for them had a quality of appreciation transcending mere words. As Myrtle was leaving, she said to him, "I am thinking of making a change."

"That's fine," he answered. "What kind of change?"

"I believe that it would be easier to do the work that is ahead of me from the invisible plane."

"Oh, you mustn't do that!" he replied. "We need your help and inspiration, your spiritual guidance here."

"You know that you will have that anyway," she said, smiling.

Significantly enough, Myrtle was instructing her secretary, Cora Dedrick, to put everything in order and was supervising many details to that end. There was a certain peace in her demeanor which seemed to indicate that inwardly she had willed to make the change.

The last Wednesday in September 1931 Myrtle led the healing meditation at the Tracy Avenue service, and on Thursday, October 1, she worked all day at the office. She was "in a gay mood," the workers said. On Friday at the farm she climbed a ladder and picked apples in the orchard.

That weekend Myrtle was ill, and on Tuesday, October 6, 1931, she slipped away to that inner side of life she knew so well.

Two weeks later at the Sunday service at Tracy Avenue Charles Fillmore took over the meditation which Myrtle had led for forty years.

Before Charles spoke the congregation knew what was in his heart. He would speak of Myrtle and his message would be one of love. Only seven months earlier Grandma Fillmore had passed on. Now Myrtle had gone, and their leader's heart seemed almost too full for words.

Charles said, "Dear friends and co-workers in Christ, it is not our custom here at Unity even to mention the visits of the 'last enemy,' whom we have resolved finally to overcome, as taught by Jesus. But there are certain conditions under which we should exchange sympathy and give thanks for that universal unity which these days of stress and strain have brought.

"I feel your sympathy and I thank you from the bottom of my heart for your expressions of comfort in thought and word.

"This occasion is so pregnant with the absence and the presence of the one who has for years stood in my place at this point in our Sunday morning lesson that I am constrained to speak a few words of consolation and comfort, not only for you but for myself.

"Personality sorrows and grieves when the bodily presence is withdrawn, but the sense of absence can be overcome when we realize that there is a spiritual bond that cannot be broken. . . . We who are following Jesus Christ in the resurrection know life as a spiritual thing, that we live spiritually if we understand the law of life, and that we shall continue to live in Spirit, 'whether in the body or out of the body.' And we know that this spiritual bond is the only bond that will really endure."

16 A New Phase

One of Charles Fillmore's literary projects was The *Metaphysical Bible Dictionary*. He turned this massive task over to a few secretaries and Bible students who were familiar with his teachings.

The preface to the dictionary, which appeared in 1931, says, "In this dictionary, Mr. Fillmore's interpretations, which have appeared in *Unity* magazine and in other Unity literature from time to time, have been used." To make the dictionary complete, Bible names which had not appeared in Unity literature were interpreted by Theodosia De Witt Schobert in consultation with Charles. There is no work of comparable length or scope (the book has over 700 pages), so that today it is the most consulted dictionary in the metaphysical field.

At this period Charles was writing another book the significance of which can hardly be understood without an appreciation of the times. In the midst of the Great Depression Charles was writing *Prosperity*.

At a time when the nation was struggling amidst the woes of unemployment and lack of money, Charles was lifting the banner of prosperity on high. Only those who lived through the agony of the depression can really know what that time of economic trial meant. For mature workers and businessmen of middle age the agony of time bedeviled the long depression. With their jobs gone, and with months and years rolling by to reduce the possibility of employment, men past middle age faced a bleak future. As one who had weathered several booms and depressions, Charles had a message for the world.

Though Charles was hard at work as founder of Unity, publisher, teacher, executive, above all he was a friend and confidant of the workers at headquarters. His friends say that there was wrapped up in his friendship the quality of exuberant life mingled with joy. "Always joy," Charles often said to May Rowland, who remembers this as one of his favorite remarks.

"Did Charles Fillmore encourage questions in all of his classes?" I once asked May Rowland.

"Yes. Sometimes he would say, 'Any more questions?' And if nobody replied he would continue, 'Any blowholes?' This usually brought laughter, but the thoroughness of his teaching was something I shall always remember."

"Do you mean," I asked, "that he always answered a question?"

"Always is a strong word," May Rowland replied. "Yes. I would say always, granting that the question was sensible! Once we had a young smart aleck in a class—you know the kind—one who jumps up at the slightest excuse to ask a question and to explain at length what he thinks ought to be explained. He kept on jumping up and asking questions and adding unneeded explanations until Charles said to him in a quiet voice, 'Just sit down until you learn something!' "

I had heard at headquarters that May Rowland had spent much time studying with Charles Fillmore, so I asked the inevitable question: "How would you describe Charles Fillmore as a teacher?"

"He was a superb teacher. I do not mean because of his class teaching merely. There was much more. He always gave his students faith—perhaps 'gave' is not the word—I should say that being a man of faith, he *imparted* faith. Again and again I heard him say to someone, 'You can do it.' One got encouragement from Charles, not merely teaching."

"May I ask you a question?" I said in the pause that followed. "Are you using the word 'faith' with reference to religion?"

"Charles often said, 'Faith is the pioneer quality of the mind,'" May Rowland replied.

"Only a pioneer could have said that!" I exclaimed.

May Rowland smiled. "Charles added experience to faith, and faith to experience. The experience that a pioneer gains gives him faith to pioneer still more. My sister Eve said to Charles once when she found that prayer had seemingly released the poisons of a disease throughout her body, 'See what has happened!'"

"No mind!" said Charles. "I have seen cancer healed. Let the prayer work."

"And your sister was healed?" I asked.

"Yes, and her faith became stronger."

"You've spoken of Charles Fillmore as a teacher," I remarked. "What was his oratorical style?"

"Charles was always careful to avoid oratory. He spoke to his audience in a natural voice, as if he were carrying on a conversation."

"Did he speak from a script?" I asked.

"Sometimes he did," May Rowland replied. "But I would say that this depended on circumstances. Sometimes he would have a script for Sunday services. Sometimes he would have only a few notes. When he was teaching a class, however, he used very few notes. As he spoke, ideas would come to him. I have seen his eyes sparkle with light when an idea came to him, and then he would speak spontaneously, with a kind of inner fire, as it were. There was a great deal of spontaneity in his teaching."

"And was he always like that? I mean, did he lecture like that up to the end?"

"Yes, Charles never ended his ministry. To think of the end of life with reference to Charles Fillmore—well, it isn't possible. You cannot think of Charles without thinking of life."

"I have heard the same thing from others who knew him," I said. "Would it be possible for you to describe how he conveyed this impression of life?"

"Well, I could describe Charles to you and yet the mere physical description would not suffice. There was a kind of gleam in his eyes —they were blue, but it wasn't so much the color in his eyes as the gleam of joy and life in them. But these are details. The essence of the matter is the impression of life that Charles gave. When you think of him an impression of life comes through—and joy, of course— always joy."

"And yet he never created the impression of—what shall I say— of holiness?"

"Heavens, no! Charles was a warm human person."

"I am looking for words to describe him," I remarked. "You see, here was a famous teacher—after all, he was famous toward the end of his life."

"Describe Charles Fillmore," May Rowland persisted, "as a warm human person."

"And a great teacher?"

"A superb teacher, yes. But Charles never let anyone put him on a pedestal. He never encouraged an atmosphere of admiration. When he felt anything like that he would always change his manner. He would tell a humorous story and break the spell, so to speak. Sometimes in class, when he felt anything of the kind, he would stop suddenly and say, 'Now let's be silent.' And he would keep us there in the silence for a long time."

"I find myself here in a kind of dilemma!" I replied. "A writer's dilemma! If I emphasize Charles as a great man, I put him on a pedestal—"

"Call him a warm human teacher, then. Sometimes I think there was a similarity between Charles Fillmore and Paul. He loved Paul, you know. He often quoted him, seemed to understand him in a unique way."

"Ah! That will help me to make Charles clear to others. Paul had a 'thorn in the flesh.' People can appreciate that! They can understand difficulties, struggles."

"Charles certainly had his struggles. He never emphasized them, but he had his full share. As you know, early in life he was crippled. But remember that through prayer he experienced the healing power of God. So he conveyed the impression of inner strength. You could see in him a man who had won his struggle.

"There were all kinds of human things about Charles," May Rowland continued. "He liked colors, so he liked to see the ladies at headquarters in bright dresses. He declared that women ought to wear cheerful colors. And if the colors were not right for the person, he would say so! Once I came to the office in a green dress, green hat, and green shoes. I was a young girl at the time, and quite pleased with the effect.

" 'Green is not your color!' " Charles declared. 'What are you wearing all that green for? Blue is your color! Yes, May, blue is better for you.' " May smiled at the remembrance. "And you never minded what he said," she continued. "You knew it was all part of his friendship."

At this my mind flashed back to a similar statement from Ernest Wilson, who had told me about a friendly exchange he once had with Charles Fillmore regarding a tie he was wearing. Evidently Charles liked colorful ties also.

"Where on earth did you get that tie?" Charles asked Ernest Wilson.

"Don't you like it?" said Ernest.

"Those colors! Where did you buy it?"

Ernest Wilson chuckled at the memory. "I had purchased it at one of the best stores downtown and it was an expensive tie. So I mentioned the name of the store. Charles grunted, and I asked, 'And where did you buy your tie, Mr. Fillmore? Those colors!'

" 'At Woolworth's!' Charles replied. And we had a good laugh together."

May Rowland nodded when I therefore said, "Yes, I have heard others speak of his love of color. I suppose," I added, "Myrtle Fillmore loved color too."

"Indeed she did. In the colors she chose for her dresses her taste was faultless. I must add that when I speak of the friendliness of Charles, I should also emphasize that Myrtle was just as friendly. Moreover, just as there was a spiritual bond between all of us and Charles so there was a similar bond between all of us and Myrtle."

May Rowland paused. "There is something else that I should say about Charles. There was a kind of wholesomeness about him that you could feel. And it was a kind of wholesomeness that made him interested in the human side of everything. He could see the human side in every situation. I never heard him criticize anybody."

Though Charles and his sons had always been close, the passing of Myrtle brought him closer than ever to Lowell and Rickert. Lowell in his unassuming way took over as much of the administrative work as possible, while Rickert often found good reasons to take his father out to the farm to discuss various projects.

Even though the work of erecting buildings on the farm had stopped because of the depression, there was much to be done. Keeping the farm up demanded time and energy. A severe drought throughout the Middle West damaged the oak and walnut trees, killing many of them outright. Rickert Fillmore had the trees felled and lumber cut for the buildings yet to come. Fifty thousand feet of black walnut lumber and thousands of feet of oak and elm were sawed into blocks and boards in a sawmill erected on the farm.

With admirable foresight Rickert planted young ash trees to make an avenue for the future plaza at Unity Farm. Today these ash trees parallel the central pool and create a pleasant avenue between the administrative buildings and the Silent Unity building.

On the one hand it may be said that Charles began to turn over the details of managing the Unity School and the task of planning Unity Farm to Lowell and Rickert; on the other hand it may be said that they lovingly took over responsibilities with Charles' consent. At this time Charles also began to encourage the people on the administrative staff to take more responsibility for their departmental work. Whenever they came to him, he gave advice as he deemed necessary, but he would often say, "You know how to solve this problem. Go ahead and work it out. You can do it."

This is one of the breaking points in the makeup of every movement—be it religious, political, academic, social, or economic. At a certain point of growth competent administrators become necessary. If they are not trained, the movement may begin to show cracks which then grow into fissures and eventually break up the original organization.

Charles was a man moving into his eighties, and he was a keen observer of life. He could trust his sons. They had found their spheres of activity. Lowell was the executive who "minded the store," and Rickert was the architect and artist who planned the move to Unity Farm and designed the buildings.

As for the department heads to whom Charles now gave freer rein —what would they do? Charles knew human nature; he could read character like a book. He knew they would make mistakes. They would probably conceive pet projects, hold fast to precious fancies, build their own artful castles, but he had taught them how to pray. He had told them, "This is the school of Jesus Christ." It was a time for Charles to have faith in his own teaching.

Charles visited Chicago in 1933, where he attended the Century of Progress to address the World Fellowship of Faiths. Ernest Wilson accompanied him, and I was glad to get intimate testimony from him on the important question of Charles Fillmore's physical healing.

"I shared a stateroom with Mr. Fillmore on the night train to Chicago," Ernest Wilson says. "It was the first time I saw him when he was not fully dressed, and I can testify that I saw with my own eyes there was no crippled, shrunken limb. The leg had filled out."

It was good to get this unexpected personal testimony, because some critics have suggested that Charles Fillmore "hid" his infirmity or that he wore special shoes.

So I asked, "What kind of shoes did Mr. Fillmore wear?"

"Canvas shoes," said Ernest Wilson. "He preferred canvas shoes to leather ones. And he liked cologne. From his earliest days he used cologne—it gave him a whiff of freshness."

"That makes him right up-to-date!" I said. "Cologne is coming back now, with a lot of other special whiffy formulas for men."

"Charles talked to the World Council of Faiths about the scientific developments of the day," Ernest Wilson continued. "He brought them up-to-date on scientific developments that religious leaders hardly knew about.

"There was one unexpected event, so far as his introduction was concerned. The chairman of the meeting had a very special complimentary speech about Mr. Fillmore all prepared in order to honor him. Just before the introduction Charles said, 'I want Ernest Wilson to introduce me.'

" 'But I have a special introduction all prepared!' objected the chairman. But Charles was firm. 'No,' he said, 'I want Ernest Wilson to introduce me.' So there I was, with only a moment's notice, called upon to introduce Charles Fillmore. Of course, I couldn't object! I knew what Charles would have said because he had often said it to me: 'You can do it.' So I did it."

Charles Fillmore told his audience of religious leaders, "My aim is to prove that in developing the unseen forces of the ether, science is merely revealing the mechanical side of that realm which Jesus called the 'Kingdom of the heavens.' "

Here was Charles once more speaking of Jesus as if he knew Him personally, taking his stand before ecclesiastics and expounding a concept of Jesus not within their purview. Their Jesus was a Jesus of dogmas, a Jesus of scripture, as expounded by each sect in its own exclusive way. Their Jesus was theologically framed. Charles Fillmore's Jesus was not in that framework at all. He was the divine man in contemporary life. To use a word now made popular through electronic computers, the divine man today is "programmed" by Mind as a contemporary scientist, artist, businessman, worker. We antiquate Jesus when we think of a two-thousand-year-old figure. We make Him contemporary man, Charles maintained, when we see that Jesus spoke of the basic energies and powers and forces of the universe, forces now being made available by science.

This was an extraordinary declaration in its time. The clerics who listened to Charles Fillmore speaking so simply and clearly, without any tricks of rhetoric, knew how old he was. He looked younger, but journalists were always mentioning his age. By the time most of the clerics arrived at that age they would be regarded as doddering by their parishioners. Here he was speaking of "his aim." What aim? To prove that the unseen forces of the ether were the mechanical side of the "Kingdom of the heavens." Extraordinary!

Back in Kansas City, Charles concentrated on his writing. Forty years had passed since his first issue of *Modern Thought,* and he had produced only three books. In the course of that time he had written reams of material for the magazines, and there were bundles of other manuscripts—stenographic notes of his talks and class lectures. So Charles felt that the time had come to write, to organize all this material, and to publish books that would present his teachings in a comprehensive form. His invaluable aid in this work was Cora G. Dedrick, his secretary for many years.

Charles had never made a lecture tour of the country, though for many years Unity centers everywhere had been asking him to visit them. Now he felt that the time had come for him to launch out on such a tour.

In December 1933, after considerable thought and planning,

Charles Fillmore retired from the pulpit of the Unity Society of Practical Christianity in Kansas City. For forty years he had served as minister of the society. Some four thousand times or more he had appeared on the platform for Sunday and Wednesday services, and now he would delegate his ministry to his friend Ernest C. Wilson.

On December 31, 1933, he married Cora G. Dedrick in a quiet ceremony at Lowell's home on Unity Farm. Charles and Cora Fillmore left the next day for California, where Charles began an extensive lecture tour.

In Los Angeles at the Shrine Auditorium Charles faced seven thousand two hundred persons, the largest single crowd he had ever addressed. (His radio listeners had numbered more, but they had been invisible.) James Dillet Freeman says that after watching the people from behind the stage curtain Charles went out to face them and said, "I feel like a little boy away from home."

They may have been surprised to see a slender, gentle person of medium height, with a cherubic smile—orators often come in imposing packages—but they took Charles to their hearts. When he finished his speech they gave him a standing ovation. "He had to be hurried out of the press of his well-wishers," James Freeman reports.

San Jose was next in Charles' tour, then San Francisco. In both cities he gave a number of talks and turned the proceeds over to the sponsoring Unity centers. Late in the spring of 1934 Charles and Cora returned to Kansas City.

17 Administrator, Lecturer, Author

That summer of 1933 Charles divided his time between Tracy Avenue and Unity Farm. At Tracy Avenue he still kept his weather eye on the course of Unity and the trend of events. At Unity Farm he spent his time writing and teaching the students at the training school. Here again Charles chose his priorities with care, for he had always considered this class important. Among the students were men and women who would be ministers in Unity centers throughout the country and they should be well taught. Charles spent much time discoursing on the metaphysical interpretation of the Bible.

That winter Charles and Cora made an automobile lecture tour throughout the Northeast. Many travelers his age might have found such a tour exhausting. Charles enjoyed every hour of it; he was interested in everything. He found tourist cabins comfortable enough, and he liked having picnic lunches along the road. He was chauffeured by a ministerial student, who was constantly being surprised by the things Papa Charles enjoyed.

Charles changed his sleeping habits when traveling, reversing his usual day and night procedure. He had always been a late worker, writing, studying, and meditating far into the early hours of the morning. Then he would snatch a few hours' sleep and wake late in the morning. On his travels he was an early riser. If they stayed in a town where no lecture was scheduled, Papa Charles went to the movies. He loved Westerns, knew the pictures that Western movie stars had made year by year, as well as their style.

Once during the tour someone fixed pillows in the back seat of the automobile for him to lie down in the afternoon and nap. When Charles saw the pillows, he asked what they were for.

"For me?" he exclaimed. "No, thank you! Take them out! I like to sit up. Besides, this is beautiful country, and I want to enjoy it."

Of course Cora acquiesced. She took consummate care of Charles, always in such a delicate way that Papa Charles never seemed conscious of her forethought and consideration.

On one of their later tours in Florida they stopped at a tourist inn, where they stayed in a cottage with a large front porch. Charles walked all around the porch, stood back from it, liked it, and decided that he wanted a house with such a porch. So he measured the porch at once, sat up late that night planning his new house, and before he went to bed he wrote a letter to a builder in Lee's Summit, giving him all the necessary details. At the same time he gave orders to the builder to start construction right away.

When Charles and Cora returned from Florida the house was ready. It was built on property owned by Cora, in pleasant wooded hills on "Unity Ridge," a quarter of a mile from Unity Farm. Here Charles lived for the rest of his career.

Very soon Papa Charles added apartments over the garage for some of the young people employed at Unity. These young men and women enlivened the Fillmore house, sitting around the hearth with Papa Charles far into the night. They chatted, laughed, questioned Papa Charles, listened to his friendly replies, and prayed with him.

Vera Dawson Tait, head of the correspondence school, remembers one evening when this quality of friendship in Charles touched her deeply.

"I was a young girl," she says, "and I had been very active during the day. That night with some friends I visited Charles and Cora

Fillmore at their home on Unity Ridge. I can remember how tired I was, and how peaceful the room was with Papa Charles in his rocking chair before the fire, chatting now and then, lapsing occasionally into silence.

"To me Papa Charles was a respected figure. I thought of him as a person far, far above me. I never asked him questions. I would never think of doing that! I let those who were closer to him ask all the questions. I was only a young girl in the group, anyway, and I had so much to learn I wasn't even sure I belonged there."

Vera paused for a long time. I could see her searching for words. Finally she continued: "So I sat on the floor near the fire, close to Papa Charles, and kept quiet. As I said, I was tired, and I fell asleep. Presently I woke up with the nicest feeling of warmth and happiness, and Papa Charles was stroking my hair gently. His touch was so light, and so human, and so gentle, and so comforting. I cannot describe that gentle touch. It gave me peace. And nicest of all was the realization that this man was my friend—not a remote Papa Charles, the great teacher, but a real human friend."

Prosperity, the book on which Charles had been working for some time, appeared in 1936. The Middle West was still hard hit by the depression. When the book is seen in the framework of our national history it gains a new and vital meaning. Charles Fillmore was not writing a mere metaphysical treatise; what he was writing was bone of his bone. The mental blood and sweat he had shed over depressions in the past had built a hardiness into his frame, and it was a hardiness that claimed divine supply as man's prerogative.

It was not an easy book to understand, particularly because of the hoity-toity idea then current in religious, mystical, and occult circles that money was a secular thing, outside the orbit of spiritually minded persons. So the ecclesiastically minded, the mystically inclined, and metaphysically oriented people dismissed the book as another one of those presentations dealing with the unspiritual topic of how to "attract money" through psychological affirmations.

They could hardly have been further from the truth. Charles wrote: "Every thought of personal possession must be dropped out of mind before men can come into the realization of the invisible supply."

The book stressed spiritual substance—not money. Out of spiritual substance wealth comes, Charles maintained. He wished to lift men out of the popular thought regarding money into a realm of comprehension regarding the source of wealth.

Again and again in his book Charles emphasized that prosperity is gained by using one's faculties creatively. He wrote, "You must use your talent, whatever it may be, in order to increase it."

This book showed Charles as a pioneer of thought in the most difficult secular field in the world. It is a book which has helped countless men and women to gain freedom from want. It is the book of a man who demonstrated his theories with remarkable success, the book of a movement which prospers today because its ideas are practiced by Unity leaders.

The year 1936 was a full one for Charles inasmuch as it also marked the publication of another book, *Mysteries of Genesis*. Its concentration on Genesis does not limit the scope of the work, for like all his other books it is wide-ranging. Here again the Christ is central. "Jehovah-Mind is the Christ-Mind," Charles declared.

Perhaps the inner significance of the book can be grasped if its title is rephrased: *Mysteries of Generation*, i.e., the generation of ideas, the world of ideas being recognized as causative and the world of manifestation being regarded as effect. The Biblical patriarchs are presented not merely as persons but as states of consciousness. Body, mind, soul, thoughts, ideas, the faculties of man, and the powers of divine Mind are elucidated through metaphysical interpretations.

In the spring of 1937 Charles plunged into administrative work at Tracy Avenue. Dr. Marcus Bach speaks of meeting Charles Fillmore in the fall of that year.

"He opened the copper-grilled door of 917 Tracy Avenue and I was impressed by the competence of his hands as he swung the door open for me. It was raining lightly at the time and he slipped out his tongue like a little boy to catch the raindrops. I could not have guessed his age, nor did I think of it at the time. Later a little calculation from his birthdate told me he was eighty-three. His manner was energetic. His firm jaws indicated strength, and I remember noticing his large ears. They were listening ears, catching sounds eagerly and grasping their meaning. It seemed to me that he listened with inner ears; the outer ears merely expressed an inner capacity to listen and understand."

Dr. Bach went on to say, "You would not have noticed that he limped ever so slightly. Had you heard that as the result of an accident to his hip seventy years ago one leg had become three inches shorter than the other and that the doctors had given him up, your only reaction would be that he had been healed somehow—healed miraculously or healed somehow."

Dr. Bach in his book *The Unity Way of Life* says, "I was always looking for miracles in those days, confident that when I found them I would be able to prove that they did not exist. It was in this contradictory spirit that I first met Charles Fillmore, and it was because of this that this man of Unity intrigued me at the time."

And ever since, it might be added. Today, thirty-five years later, Dr. Marcus Bach still regards the ideals of Unity with admiration and he conducts a column, "Questions on the Quest," for *Unity* magazine.

In 1939 Charles Fillmore's book *Jesus Christ Heals* appeared. It was his sixth book, and once again Charles returned to his original theme as presented in his first book, *Christian Healing*. It was as if he were saying, "Now let us return to basics. I shall elaborate more on the theme of healing." So he said, "As Jesus healed in Galilee so He is healing in the same spiritual realm of radiant health today."

It was an extraordinary statement in its way, not extraordinary insofar as the name Jesus is concerned, but insofar as most Christian churches were concerned. They called upon the name of Jesus for sacraments and for the saving of the soul, but at that time in the 1930s most churches paid little attention to spiritual healing. A few courageous innovators in the churches were holding services, but their approach was tentative, even though spiritual healing had come into being in the last half of the nineteenth century through metaphysical movements.

In the 1970s *Jesus Christ Heals* is still a pioneering book. Many of its statements about the body, the mind, and thought are still regarded as startling. For instance: "If God is Spirit and He dwells in man's body, that body must have within it certain spiritual principles. Here modern science comes to the rescue of primitive Christianity, telling us that the atoms that compose the cells of our body have within them electrical units that, released, can change the whole character of the organism."

Other statements in the book reveal Charles Fillmore as a farseeing prophet of world events yet to come. Appearing in 1939, the text must have been written a year or so earlier. Charles had been traveling on lecture tours for the preceding two winters, and during the intervening summers he had carried on his administrative work at Tracy Avenue.

In any case Hitler's invasion of Poland on September 1, 1939, started a series of world events which Charles Fillmore had foreseen a year or two earlier when he was writing *Jesus Christ Heals*. Here again the knowledge displayed by Charles of international and national events reveals his sensitivity to world trends.

He quoted the sixth chapter of Revelation regarding "four horses and their riders," noting first the appearance of a white horse, symbolizing the Christ, and of three subsequent horses: a red horse (war); a black horse (commercialism); and a pale horse (death).

"At no time in the history of the world has there ever been such activity in the riders of the three dark horses as right now. The prodigious preparations for war by nations, incited by the greed for gain, will soon lead them to 'let slip the dogs of war' unless the rider of the white horse comes forth 'conquering, and to conquer.'

"Although all Truth students are praying for harmony in the settlement of earth's tribulations, they cannot help seeing the effect of thoughts of selfishness. The last section of this chapter of Revelation gives a symbolic description of the chaos to come among those who are not seeking to conquer under the banner of the white horse, Christ."

"The chaos to come," Charles prophesied two years before Hitler invaded Poland and started the series of invasions which led to World War II.

The construction of a new Unity temple in Kansas City had been delayed because of the depression and because of the expense involved in maintaining Unity Farm. Ernest C. Wilson had waited patiently for funds.

"I spoke to Charles Fillmore about it several times," Ernest Wilson says, "and asked for money to begin building the temple. But Charles would reply that Unity Farm should come first and that there would be enough money for both in the end."

Charles proved himself a practical businessman in this matter, with a sense of priorities characteristic of all good executives. The author of *Prosperity* was no dreamy idealist inclined to scatter money in all directions because he had written: "When you work in harmony with this universal Law, every needed thing is abundantly supplied." He knew that right use must go with right supply, and his friends honored him for his recognition of priorities.

Four years after his appointment as minister in Kansas City, Ernest Wilson accepted a call from a Unity center in Los Angeles, where he founded Christ Church, Unity. Louis E. Meyer was then appointed minister to replace Ernest Wilson, and at last in 1940, twelve years after Charles had purchased the lot for a new Unity temple on the outskirts of the city, construction began.

The open country where goats were accustomed to feed when Charles bought the lot had become a development called Country Club Plaza. When Charles bought this parcel of land he had not lost his touch as a real-estate operator. Country Club Plaza was a booming development, one of the most promising in the Middle West.

Since the cost of the project was great—more than a million dollars, a great deal of money in those days—it was decided that the temple should be built in stages. First the Sunday school rooms were built and furnished. This action was a tribute to Myrtle Fillmore, who had always considered her work with children of prime importance. Finally in 1950 Rev. Louis E. Meyer completed the sanctuary, which seats fifteen hundred.

Today Unity Temple in Country Club Plaza rises among some of the most attractive buildings in Kansas City and adds its architectural beauty to some of the finest buildings in town.

Today it is well to note also, as characteristic of the honor Unity School pays its tried workers, that the Reverend Mr. Meyer is chaplain at Unity School headquarters in Unity Village, while the Reverend Mr. Wilson has returned to Kansas City as minister of the Unity Temple.

Charles Fillmore's fifth book, *Teach Us to Pray*, was published in 1941. The title page reads: "By Charles and Cora Fillmore." Remarks made later by Cora indicate that the book is an amplification of stenographic notes which she made during Charles' lectures and discussions on prayer. Many of the chapters are short dissertations, so that the book is not a formal treatise. It is more in the nature of a bedside book for those who enjoy a few inspiring pages before retiring at night. There are passages of keen spiritual insight and startling metaphysical statements. Charles says: "So the Christian who thinks he is saved when he has been 'converted' will find that his salvation has just begun. Conversion and 'change of heart' are real experiences, as anyone who has passed through them will testify, but they are merely introductory to the new life in Christ."

As always the keynote of love for Jesus Christ resounds throughout the book.

In every century there have been a few keen disciples who have felt a precious, intimate, personal relationship with Jesus. For instance, in the sixteenth century George Herbert "used in his ordinarie speech, when he made mention of . . . Jesus Christ, to adde, *My Master*."*

In George Herbert's poem, "The Odour," this feeling of his is expressed in an exquisite verse:

> How sweetly doth *My Master* sound! *My Master!*
> As Amber-greese leaves a rich scent
>   Unto the taster:
> So do these words a sweet content,
> An orientall fragrancie, *My Master*.

In our century Charles Fillmore was one of this rare band of disciples. For him Jesus was always *"Master."*

Vera Tait says that Ida Palmer, an early Unity teacher, often repeated a prayer that Charles would say at the beginning of a class: "Jesus Christ, my Teacher, my Healer, reveal Thyself in me and through me."

Thus Charles could write in *Teach Us to Pray*: "When we pray in the name of the Lord Jesus Christ, we decree His presence and power in our spiritual work, we effect a reunion with His supermind and its tremendous ramifications in heaven and earth, and our own meager spiritual ability is augmented a thousandfold."

*Elizabeth Waterhouse, Ed., *A Little Book of Life and Death*.

18 "Do You See the New Jerusalem?"

When the attack on Pearl Harbor came on December 7, 1941, profound national issues changed the country overnight. Unity felt the effects in many ways. The construction work at Unity Farm was suspended, though the operation of the farm itself as an agricultural unit became important. One section of the farm became a huge "Victory Garden" for members of the staff and their associates.

With World War II at its height there were strict building limitations and laws to be obeyed, but Rickert Fillmore was an ingenious builder, imbued with his father's vision. There were limestone quarries to be worked, building blocks to be cut. There was sand for cement. There was wood for beams to be cut from trees killed during the great drought of the 1930s.

Rickert Fillmore brought prefabrication to a fine art on the farm. He erected a "casting building" and built sections of concrete. Much of the stone trim in the buildings today consists of concrete cast into molds, with color judiciously added to harmonize with the Italian Renaissance architecture.

In 1942 the librarian at Unity headquarters, Pharaby Boileau, discovered the "Covenant" signed by Charles and Myrtle Fillmore. The Covenant was among some old papers of Myrtle's; the writing, in Charles' hand, was clear and strong. Fifty years had elapsed since the signing of the Covenant in 1892. Those who knew the stringent financial circumstances prevailing at the time of the Covenant were deeply moved by its discovery. Today it is read in an affluent society with little understanding of the faith and dedication needed during that time of financial difficulty.

Charles' eighth book, *Mysteries of John*, appeared in 1946. Thus he joined that admiring circle of mystics down through the ages who have found the Gospel of John uniquely inspiring. Clement of Alexandria, one of the early church fathers, called it "the spiritual gospel." Dean W. R. Inge of St. Paul's in his book *Christian Mysticism* had called it "the charter of Christian mysticism." He had declared with emphasis, "For we cannot but feel that there are deeper truths in this wonderful Gospel than have yet become part of the religious consciousness of mankind."

Probably Charles would have said, "Not only the Fourth Gospel, but the teachings of Jesus have not yet become part of the religious consciousness of mankind." In fact he said as much again and again throughout his books. In *Mysteries of John* Charles continued the metaphysical interpretation of names as the expression of divine qualities. pointing out that Biblical personages truly manifest the qualities which their names symbolize.

A profound knowledge of human psychology pervaded the book. For instance, Charles explained the cleansing of the temple (John 2:14-16) as symbolic of the cleansing of the body. In this process, he declared, the student must use a "scourge of small cords" to formulate his words or statements of denial. Then with cleansing honesty Charles declares: "When we deny in general terms we cleanse the consciousness, but secret sins may yet lurk in the inner parts. The words that most easily reach these errors are not great ones, such as 'I am one with Almightiness; my environment is God' but small, definite statements that cut like whipcords into the sensuous, fleshly mentality."

And again, "Excessive zeal in observing the forms of religious worship eats up the truly spiritual. When we become very zealous in observing the rites of the church, we are prone to forget the church itself, which is Christ''.

Very early in his career Charles Fillmore declared that he would do his best to follow Jesus in overcoming death, and from that moment he was bombarded with unbelieving questions, some of them impolite, others scornful and even derisive. Had Charles kept silent about this declaration after the first few years of astonished public reaction, he would have made things easier for himself.

In the world of esoteric teaching and yogic tradition the possibility of overcoming death is accepted as the logical end of spiritual achievement here on earth. Esoteric students who know that there are a few true adepts here on earth manifesting this degree of attainment say very little about this matter. In yoga the body thus attained is called "the body of yoga," or "the body of light." Yogins and advanced disciples who have arrived at this stage have been known to a few students both in the Orient and the Occident, nowadays and in the past.

This is the ultimate stage of attainment, however, and yogins and esoteric students believe that it is best not to talk about it since the subject introduces too many mind-shaking problems and unimaginable concepts at the present stage of human consciousness. Moreover, any advanced student who approaches this stage and speaks about it brings upon himself the scorn and derision of the masses, with consequences that may make his own achievement difficult.

From a certain point of view the reaction of the public, and of some Truth students, to Charles' declaration of intent is a sad commentary on theological Christianity. The Master Christian, as Charles pointed out insistently, had resurrected His body. Paul himself had seen the possibility for himself, writing to the Phillipians about the power of Christ's resurrection and saying, "If by any means I might attain unto the resurrection of the dead" (Phil. 3:11).

Thomas Troward, who influenced New Thought in Great Britain, was a profound Bible student, and in one of his books, *The Law and the Word,* he specifically declared that Paul was "here not speaking of a general 'resurrection of the dead,' but as the word *exanastasis* in the original Greek indicates, of a special resurrection from among the dead; this indicates an *individual* achievement, not merely something common to the race."

To Judge Troward, dean of the New Thought movement in Great Britain, this kind of body-transformation was a logical possibility—indeed it was the fulfillment of Jesus Christ's teachings, and Troward declared it was a stage which later followers would attain when Jesus' teachings were more fully grasped. Other New Thought leaders in England were of the same opinion, including Harry Gaze, who had written a book outlining the possibilities of overcoming death—*Science of Physical Immortality.*

In the United States certain New Thought leaders hinted at the possibility of physical immortality in the light of Christ's teachings and of Paul's declaration that he also hoped to attain the crown of resurrection. Charles Fillmore, however, with characteristic courage and bluntness said that he was not content to view the transformation of the body as a logical possibility and no more. "If it is logically possible," he said, "I am going to take it as my goal and achieve it. I am like Napoleon's drummer boy. I do not know how to beat a retreat and am not going to learn."

The inner teaching regarding physical immortality as found in yoga and in esoteric tradition is not so simplistic as some metaphysical students are inclined to assume. According to the teaching, physical immortality is possible only when other, higher, spiritual demands are met and fulfilled. What appears as physical immortality at a certain stage of attainment is not a final stage. It is in fact misnamed. It is in reality a step to a still higher state, the translation of the body into cosmic realms of bliss and progress.

In other words, physical immortality is not an end, but the beginning of a new and higher process that leads up to what some students call translation, or ascension. The true man is not of the earth, earthy, but of the heavens, heavenly.

It is well to note that in the very attempt to keep a physical body forever a man might separate himself from his spiritual nature and block his cosmic line of progress. At this point an open path leads upward to more advanced realms, otherwise physical immortality might turn out to be a kind of cosmic block, an exquisite hell.

The goal is not life everlasting on earth but the expression of the Christ-consciousness here on earth to the fullest degree. This fulfillment leads to "the place" of cosmic progression which Christ has prepared for His own. "In my Father's house are many mansions. . . . I go to prepare a place for you," said Jesus (John 14:2).

Charles Fillmore outlined much of this in his writings, and his books are replete with statements of this kind through various analogies and idioms.

For instance, we have noted that in his teaching about reincarnation he declared that the purpose of reincarnation was to procure this ultimate end—transformation into the spiritual realm without death. Thus he never laid emphasis on memories of incarnations or speculations along the lines of future incarnations. The wise course, he declared, is to work toward the goal and not dabble in speculations which are likely to prove bypaths.

In *Talks on Truth* Charles outlined in sharp terms what perfection of the body meant. He stated, in his original manner, that the construction of the church of Christ was no mere parable, but that it signified the construction of the perfect body.

"This means that your body will be so transformed within and without that it will never go through the change called death. It will be a resurrected body, becoming more and more refined as you catch sight of the free truth of Being, until it will literally disappear from the sight of those who see with the eye of sense."

A friend who was close to Charles said that a day or so before he passed on he remarked that he had no fear, and that next time he would return with a perfect body. Some students of these matters understand the statement to mean that the next time he would return for his last incarnation and that he would procure a perfect body, thus overcoming death and procuring his translation to higher realms. He would join the great cloud of witnesses, "the general assembly and church of the firstborn, which are written in heaven" (Heb. 12:23).

Orthodox dogma presented no open-ended line of progress to higher realms, to the "great cloud of witnesses" (Heb. 12:1) except through death. Charles Fillmore never accepted this view, and this is why he had to explain himself so often. In 1946 he was still answering questions along these lines, and he said with his usual frankness in *Unity,* "I do not claim that I have yet attained perfection but I am on my way." (How similar his words are to Paul's!) "My leg is still out of joint but it is improving as I continue to work under the direction and guidance of Spirit."

When we understand the full significance of Charles Fillmore's valiant attempt to demonstrate the highest aspects of divinity here and now, in full plenitude at this stage of human evolution, we can recognize his pioneering courage and vision. And we can say, as those who knew him said in the end, "Well done, thou good and faithful servant."

Charles spent the winter of 1947 in California, lecturing at centers on the Pacific Coast and residing at his home in the San Fernando Valley.

Rosemary Fillmore Rhea, granddaughter of Charles Fillmore, saw him often during his winter periods in California. When I interviewed her, she declared, "In everything I say about Charles Fillmore, I must make it clear that I looked upon him as my grandfather and not as a metaphysician. He was one of the most delightful people I have ever known.

"Of course, as I look back now I can see that for many people he was a spiritual teacher, the founder of a well-known movement, and so forth. I came to realize this later, but as a young girl I just knew him as my grandfather. I never thought of him as unusual. I just knew that he was warm and friendly and kind—always kind. To me he was a person whom it was nice to be with."

Rosemary paused for a moment. We were in her office on the fourth floor of Unity Tower, the headquarters of Unity Radio and Television Department.

"If you had to describe Charles Fillmore over a radio or television broadcast in a single phrase, what would you say?" I asked.

"I'd call him a nice, warm, human person."

"And if you were asked about your memories of him?"

"That would take more time! I would start as a young girl, perhaps as far back as Tracy Avenue. After the farm was bought Papa Charles was always finding excuses to take people out there for a picnic. Again and again he would say, 'Let's all go for a picnic out to the farm,' and out to the farm we'd go. He enjoyed every moment of a picnic."

Rosemary chuckled. "Oh, I must tell you this!" she exclaimed, her eyes shining with delight. "I was born at home on the farm. Papa Charles wanted me named 'Unity Farm,' and my father, Rick, had a hard time talking him out of it!"

I smiled at Rosemary's sudden change of expression. She became serious. "Of course you could have used a nickname," I ventured.

"Can you imagine the nicknames I would have been called at school—a girl named 'Unity Farm'?" Rosemary asked. "But enough of that. Papa Charles always invited me to the weddings at the farm. As a little girl I loved the cakes and cookies, and of course I always got some of the wedding cake. Well, Papa Charles would always tell me about the weddings and invite me as a guest. 'Get nicely dressed,' he would say. What I specially liked about being a guest was that I could sit down at the chicken dinners and eat chicken with the grownups. Papa Charles enjoyed my joy—you can see why I was sure he understood me!

"I was always glad when I could sit next to him at parties, or even at home. He felt good. I liked his presence. I can remember so well that if I was ill Papa Charles would come and sit by my bed. Sometimes we'd chat. He never talked metaphysics to me."

"Never?" I asked.

Rosemary searched her memory. "Never—so that I could recognize it! But after a while I would feel better. Sometimes I'd fall asleep, and when I'd wake up Papa Charles would be gone and I would be better."

"Amazing!" I murmured. "Here was a teacher who never preached at home!"

"Never!" Rosemary insisted. "He had such common sense, too, even insofar as metaphysics and physical conditions were concerned. I remember once I dislocated my knee. It was quite painful, so they called Papa Charles on the telephone and told him about it. He asked a few questions and then said, 'Get someone to give her knee a quick jerk!'" Rosemary smiled.

"And?" I queried.

"Someone who knew how—that was part of the advice!—gave my knee a jerk, and I was all right."

Rosemary was interrupted by her secretary, who came in with an urgent letter for her to sign. As she signed it she said, "Oh, yes, about Papa Charles' letters. Sometimes when he was on his trips he would write me a chatty letter. Often he would begin, 'I am writing on my knees in my bedroom.' Those letters really showed that he was fond of me.

"When I grew up and went to school in California, I did not lose contact with Papa Charles because he came out to California too. He bought a house in the San Fernando Valley near Los Angeles. He loved California, the outdoors, the freedom."

"So you were also close to him when you were growing up?"

"Yes. Growing up brought difficulties—they were my own, of course. For instance, there came a time when I no longer went to the movies with him. He loved Westerns, you know. He saw every

Western he could. Well, young men took me to the movies, instead, and that was to be expected, but I began to go with someone whom I knew Papa Charles would not approve of as a constant companion. Oh, he never said so—he never uttered a word about it. Yet I knew how he felt."

Rosemary paused for a moment in deep thought. "Of course this was all a part of my growing up. Come to think of it, I wouldn't pass through my growing-up period again for anything! To return to Papa Charles . . . he was always interested in everything I did. When I graduated from the drama school in California I was in radio for a while. Papa Charles said to me, 'You will be in the movies.' But movies didn't work out for me and I kept on wondering about his remark. Now I am in television, so you see he was right. There was no television in those days, but he certainly saw something."

"Did you see him much when you were in California?"

"A good deal. I planned to take an important step at one time and spoke to Papa Charles about it. He said, 'Spirit has told me that it is not the right thing for you to do,' but he did not press the matter. He gave me no further advice and never mentioned the topic again. He left me perfectly free. Of course my feelings were hurt.

"I went ahead and followed my inclination, anyway, and it did not turn out right for me. I never discussed the situation with Papa Charles again, but I knew him well and knew what he thought. He didn't have to tell me. Let me hasten to add we were always the best of friends. As I look back now I see that I was just growing up."

"May I return to Papa Charles as the founder of Unity?" I asked. "When you grew up you must have become conscious of him as the leader of a great movement. You said you did not think of him as a metaphysician at first—"

"I don't suppose I ever really regarded him from that point of view. He was my grandfather, and I was glad he was—that's how I felt."

"Yes, but forgive me," I persisted. "Here was a famous teacher. You were in California—you know what I mean when I say here was a great Guru, a holy man!"

"No—no! He never took that stand! Never at any time would he let anyone offer him personal admiration. He would make a joke, change the conversation, tell a story, turn the admiration aside. I saw him do that more than once." Rosemary knitted her brows in thought.

She took her time about speaking, then said, "I would put it this way. He could never accept the 'holy man' pedestal because he never thought that way. He never seemed self-conscious. He lost his self-consciousness before I knew him."

I remained silent, thinking that this was the highest praise for a spiritual teacher that I had ever heard. Throughout many years in the field of religious movements and metaphysical schools I have known many teachers, and even some Gurus, who were not averse to being known as holy men. I had never found anyone who had lost his self-consciousness before I met him.

I wanted to close the interview on that note. "Thank you—" I began.

"One thing more," said Rosemary quietly. "Just one thing more to give you a true picture. In all my life I never knew Papa Charles to have any unpleasant personality relationships."

During the 1940s Charles divided his time between California and Missouri. In the summers he returned to Unity Farm, teaching classes, visiting headquarters at Tracy Avenue, and keeping a captain's eye out to note the course of Unity.

At this time, when he was in his nineties, Charles wrote one of his best-known affirmations in clear, strong script:

"I fairly sizzle with zeal and enthusiasm and I spring forth with a mighty faith to do the things that ought to be done by me."

In the late fall of 1947 Charles returned to California for a series of lectures. He ceased his lectures in February 1948 because he was unwell, returning to his home at Unity Farm in April.

Except for that other occasion in 1919 when he was ill, Charles had never taken to his bed. Now he remained quietly in bed, sleeping much, talking to his family and friends when he was awake.

He still liked a good story. He smiled and enjoyed witticisms, showed his appreciation with a few words, a nod of his head, an engaging smile.

Cora Dedrick Fillmore took exquisite care of him. "Read to me about divine Love," he would say to her. "I have always been a man of action. I need the comfort that comes from resting in Love."

So Cora read to him much of the time, often from stenographic notes of his own talks or from his own manuscripts.

"It was so wonderful," Cora would say later, "to have him exclaim 'That's good! I can see that!' or 'That's logical! Who wrote that?' "

"Why, you did, Charles!" Cora would reply, and they would both smile.

During a friend's visit he suddenly asked, "Do you know what the most important words in the world are?"

"No, what are they, Papa Charles?"

"Christ in you, the hope of glory." After a moment of silence he joyfully repeated twice, "Christ in you, the hope of glory."

Near the end he said, "It looks like I'll have to go, but don't worry, I'll be back." Once he declared, "I am going to have a new body, anyway, and this time it's going to be a perfect body."

His going gave him no concern. "I am facing it," he said, "but I am not afraid of it."

The last day or so Charles Fillmore had a recurring vision. "Do you see it? Do you see it?" he would ask, staring intently upward. It was the inner vision he had beheld all his life. "Don't you see it? The New Jerusalem, coming down from God, the new heaven and the new earth."

On the morning of July 5, 1948, Charles awoke from sleep. He saw Lowell, who was constantly at his side, smiled, and was gone.

Epilogue

With a prescience unrealized by his friends until the time came for his purpose to unfold, Charles Fillmore had trained competent leaders to carry on his work. He had been doing this for several years, and now Unity was safe with the men and women he had chosen.

The wisdom of his teaching was soon evident. Often when the head of a religious group or a metaphysical school dies, divisions arise between the assistants, dissident groups form, egotistical voices seek a hearing, disciples drift away. Nothing of the kind happened; Unity did not break into parts. No division arose among the assistants Charles Fillmore had trained, no dissident groups formed, no egotistical voice sounded a discordant note, no disciple broke away to start a separate movement.

Those who come to Unity Village often speak of it as a bit of heaven on earth. Again and again, mingling with visitors I have been able to hear this sentiment expressed by people who speak spontaneously to other visitors. One summer afternoon I sat near the bridge over the central pool with a group of people who invited me to join them to see the sunset. I thanked them, remarking that I found such friendliness enjoyable.

"You know," said a gentleman with a southern drawl, waving his hand toward the fountain and the buildings of Unity Village, "all this is the working out of a prophecy. Charles Fillmore used to say so. How happy he must have been to see his dream realized."

At that moment I felt a pang. It was gone in an instant, for one should feel no sense of pain in connection with Charles Fillmore. Yet it had come, for in that moment I realized that Charles had never seen Unity Village. He had seen only the Tower and the Silent Unity building, its exterior decoration not yet complete. The long pool which the bridge spanned had been a farm pond when Charles walked these acres. The ash trees were mere saplings planted by Rickert to indicate the lines of the future plaza. The magnificent buildings now reflecting the sunset sky were not there.

Yet there was no need for any human pang. Charles Fillmore had beheld Unity Farm with the luminous inner vision of prophecy. These buildings might have made him glad, but even so his vision would transcend all these things. "Have joy," he often said to his friends. His vision and his joy were one: Manifestation flowed from them, and he kept the source pure.

Today Unity Village is renowned, drawing visitors from all parts of the world. Unity Farm, now Unity Village, covers 1,400 acres, as compared with the original 38 acres.

In 1949, a year after his passing, Charles' book *Atom-Smashing Power of Mind* was published. In this book Charles again emphasized the fact that the discoveries of science were also metaphysical discoveries and that they unveiled the energies and powers of "the ethers," the Kingdom of the heavens. In this book he quoted Sir Francis Galton, Sir James Jeans, Robert Andrews Millikan, and other scientists. Several chapters in the book had been published in *Unity* over a period of years.

The release of atomic energy through fission was no surprise to Charles. For years he had been writing about the transformation of body-energies through the mind, and for him the atomic bomb was the explosive manifestation of this energy. He wrote: "People the world over were amazed and terrified when they read of the destruction wrought on the cities and people of Japan by two atomic bombs. But do we realize that millions of people are killed every year by atomic force? Doctors tell us that it is the toxin generated in our own bodies that kills us."

Then Charles went on to say that it must be our own minds that produce this toxic force! He declared that disease germs are "the manifested results of anger, revenge, jealousy, fear, impurity, and many other mind activities." This, of course, is on the negative side —on the positive side thoughts of truth produce positive changes within the body. "When the white heat of God-life comes upon man there is exaltation and transfusion of elements. The result of soul exaltation is a finer soul essence forming the base of a new body substance."

Atom-Smashing Power of Mind is still a pioneer in its field. From the first issue of *Modern Thought* in 1889 Charles sought to harmonize the discoveries of science with the teachings of Jesus. The attempt was viewed without favor by churchmen on the one hand and by scientists on the other. Clergymen in those days were untaught in the rudiments of science and sought no link between religion and science. Scientists on their part sought no link because of the attacks of theologians on the scientific teachings of the day. Now in the 1970s the possibility of building a bridge between science and religion is gaining ground, and Charles Fillmore's prophetic vision is slowly coming to pass.

Apart from his concept of the close relationship between the truths of religion and science, Charles Fillmore also emphasized other truths which churchmen are beginning to envision. Instead of declaring that a man must die in order to gain the kingdom of heaven, he declared that man must live in the kingdom of heaven now. The concepts of a punitive God and of damnation induce fear in worshipers, impeding a man's spiritualization. Instead of presenting a punitive God, Charles presented a God who was too intelligent and loving to be punitive. Instead of speaking of damnation, Charles

spoke of life everlasting here and now. He pointed out that these
were the true teachings of Jesus. Modern, intelligent men and women
find these teachings intelligent and relevant to our human condition;
hence the growth of Unity.

In the more successful churches today ministers are no longer
stressing the old theological dogmas. They might almost be described
as going the Unity way—not because these ministers are opportun-
ists, but because they are a new breed of men who speak to the
contemporary mind in relevant terms.

Because Charles Fillmore began to teach in this way at the end of
the last century, he deserves recognition as a pioneer of thought.

Of course our present religious climate is by no means due to the
work of Charles Fillmore alone. Such an assertion would be both
pompous and foolish. The religious climate has been affected by
metaphysical teachers, New Thought leaders, teachers and Gurus
from the East, occult and esoteric teachers—all of whom stress
teachings that have cleared the air of rigid theological dogma.
Charles Fillmore was one of the first of this pioneer band, and even
among them he was a man of rank.

Well-known writers and speakers like Dr. Norman Vincent Peale
and Dr. Emmet Fox have said that Charles Fillmore profoundly influenced their lives. Eric Butterworth, a friend of both of these pastors, says, "Dr. Norman Vincent Peale came to Unity Village at the
time of our seventy-fifth anniversary in 1964 to deliver an address,
and in the course of his speech he said that he had been an orthodox
preacher, just rolling along, until Charles Fillmore's writings came
into his life. He studied his writings, and a great change followed in
his thinking. He saw the positive side of Christ's mission in a new
light. Soon his sermons became more vital and dynamic."

"Are you speaking of the author of *The Power of Positive Thinking?*" I asked.

"Yes. The book topped the best-seller list for months. As a matter
of fact the phrase 'positive thinking' came from Charles Fillmore, as
Dr. Peale openly declared."

"Perhaps Charles Fillmore should have copyrighted the phrase!" I remarked.

Eric Butterworth smiled. "Charles never copyrighted anything. He declared that ideas could not be copyrighted and that anyone could quote him freely, or could use without hindrance anything he had written."

Eric Butterworth paused for a moment. "Then there was Dr. Emmet Fox, whom I knew very well," he continued. "He came to Unity Village often when I was there. He had been an engineer by profession in England, but the ideas of Charles Fillmore influenced him so profoundly that he changed his profession. Emmet Fox also declared that he was a spiritual child of Charles Fillmore.

"To my knowledge, many other pastors and teachers have been benefited by Charles Fillmore's writings. During my last trip to England when I visited an Episcopalian [Anglican] minister I noticed the books of Charles Fillmore in his study. My casual inquiry brought this reply: 'I may be an Episcopalian priest, but I am a student of Charles Fillmore.' "

"Let us consider another aspect of Charles Fillmore's teachings," I suggested. "For instance, his original ideas regarding the body. You have written some articles on Charles Fillmore as a prophet of modern science, and I know that required a great deal of research."

"In a way, yes. I have spent many years studying this question, collecting data and following the latest scientific discoveries. It is possible to show that one scientific discovery after another was anticipated by him. And it is possible to document each case of his 'prevision' from his writings. A whole volume could be written on this subject."

"A whole volume?" I echoed, conscious that I already had enough information on Charles Fillmore to fill one book.

Eric Butterworth must have sensed my writer's dilemma, for he laughed heartily. "At least," he said, "a good history is a good beginning."

The history of a man has two aspects: events as they appeared to him, and the same events as they appeared to others. When Charles was asked to write about himself for the booklet *Unity's Fifty Golden Years,* he wrote a short chapter entitled "Confidentially." He was then eighty-five. He touched lightly on the "many small and uninteresting matters that are common to most persons," and declared: "Consulting the light of Spirit, I have been privileged to see states of consciousness formed by my ego thousands of years before its entry into this body, and I must measure the present status of myself not only by what the conscious mind registers but what is stored up in the subconscious pigeonholes or brain pockets. So let us understand that we are taking notes of the minor episodes of an ego whose real identity has been veiled by sense in much of its history but is now being cleared up by the light of Spirit."

In this biography I have left out "minor episodes," not only for reasons of space, but for reasons of perspective in accordance with Charles' point of view. A few of these minor aspects, however, may be touched upon for obvious reasons. People say, "Yes, but the man was human. Where was he inconsistent? What mistakes did he make?"

Now inconsistency, even more than beauty, is in the eye of the beholder. There is an inconsistency of greatness and an inconsistency of smallness; all men can be proved inconsistent at one time or another. The inconsistency of greatness appears when a choice is made for a higher principle not hitherto in prospect. The inconsistency of smallness has no principle but varies with every wind. As for mistakes, after the dust of events settles it is easy to trace a leader's course and say he should have gone this way instead of that, but blaming the man is tantamount to blaming the dust of events.

Mistakes become important when they are not corrected. The downfall of a great man begins when he no longer corrects his mistakes. Every man who succeeds in life corrects his mistakes as he goes along, just as a navigator corrects his course against wind and tide. The course of his life then indicates how effectively his corrections have been made.

Whenever Charles Fillmore discovered a mistake, he corrected it smoothly. Sometimes it was a happenstance in a province hitherto unexplored, such as the "red leaf" incident. This leaf was a sheet colored deep red, imprinted with the "Class Thoughts," or prayers being used by Silent Unity, and bound in the magazine *Unity*.

Some subscribers began to tear out the red leaf with its prayer and to apply it to parts of their bodies. They reported healing as a result, and the red leaf practice caught on among some eager subscribers. Charles wrote in *Unity* that there was no mysterious virtue in the page, the virtue being in the prayer, uttered with faith and diligence.

The practice continued, however, and it brought some sardonic publicity, but Charles was not disturbed. Later he discontinued the red leaf, but he did so with a gentleness that brought no slightest disturbance to the faith of any student of Unity. He graciously led many of his followers out of the valley of reliance on physical tokens to the mountaintop of dependence on pure prayer.

Charles Fillmore was often accused of borrowing. It was characteristic of him not to deny the charge, but to reply with astonishing frankness, "I have taken the best in all religions and brought them all together in the light of Jesus Christ's teachings."

Even so, a comparison between Charles' presentations and the teachings of other schools leaves one impressed with his originality, rather than his "borrowing." For instance, it is possible to compare the body-centers described in *The Twelve Powers of Man* with the chakras or centers as described in yoga. But closer study reveals that Charles delineates faculties of mind and states of consciousness which transform the ancient yoga into a contemporary metaphysical presentation. There is a different polarization.

It is even possible to trace in Swedenborg's theory of correspondences some of the relationships found by Charles between mental faculties—the disciples—and the body-centers. Because of his comprehensive study of religious systems, Charles was probably acquainted with these ideas, but he used their gold to mint new coin

—obverse and reverse—stamped with inscriptions of contemporary value for his students.

Again, it is possible to trace in some of Charles Fillmore's teachings a similarity to certain Rosicrucian ideas and other esoteric traditions. As one familiar in a degree with these systems it is my opinion after extensive study that so much ingenuity and so many presumptions are called for in order to locate "sources" that the explication becomes an intellectual tour de force which merely reveals skill on the part of the researcher. A researcher may show how clever he is, but legerdemain is not truth.

L. E. Meyer quotes a pertinent statement of Charles which had a profound influence on his life.

"Mr. Fillmore often said to me," he declares, " 'True ideas have only One Source and One Giver.' "

For this reason Charles Fillmore is not excessively quoted today by Unity teachers and ministers. Trained to turn to the One Source of ideas, they express thoughts that they have made their own. They do not consider themselves as a group of teachers or ministers pledged to the furtherance of Charles Fillmore's fame, but as teachers who propound truth in the idiom of the day for the furtherance of practical Christianity.

Undoubtedly the name of Charles Fillmore would be better known, his fame would be more widespread, and his importance as a pioneer of thought would be more fully recognized if Unity ministers and Unity centers and churches were assiduous in promoting his name. But Charles Fillmore would not have it otherwise.

On one occasion when some students arranged a program to honor Charles and Myrtle, they invited them to the meeting without indicating its purpose. When the Fillmores arrived, a flattering address was started, and other students took up the refrain.

As soon as Charles realized what the purpose of the meeting was, he rose to his feet and said, "Why callest thou me good? None is good, save one, that is, God."

Then he started them singing a well-known hymn and changed the meeting into a hymnfest in praise of God.

The total literary and teaching output of Charles Fillmore was colossal. In addition to his books there are his miscellaneous writings for over fifty years: editorials in Unity magazines such as *Modern Thought, Unity, Weekly Unity, Good Business, Progress.* (All of these magazines are now combined in *Unity.*) Of course there are other articles in addition to his editorials, including his earliest writings under his pen name, Leo-Virgo. Add his class lectures, many of which have been preserved through stenographic notes, and we have a vast collection of material.

In the Heritage Library at Unity Village there are also several drawers packed with unpublished manuscripts of Charles Fillmore. Neatly typed by Cora Dedrick Fillmore, they await detailed analysis. Sample studies have been made, and these indicate that many of the topics are covered in his books. Someday these writings may be published, and in the end there may be a massive concordance. Thus the eleven books available to the public today under the name of Charles Fillmore constitute a very small percentage of his life output.

Charles Fillmore's family relationships, always blessed, have also proved a blessing to Unity. Today Lowell Fillmore is president emeritus of the Unity School of Christianity, after a lifetime of dedicated service. His presence at headquarters every day is a remarkable proof of his love for the movement. Every morning he "makes the rounds," and he may often be found in a friend's office, his presence a recognition of the profound fellowship at Unity headquarters.

Rickert Fillmore's son, Charles Rickert Fillmore, is now president of Unity School, guiding the affairs of Unity with all the efficiency to be expected of a contemporary business executive, but at the same time expressing the warm interest in people so characteristic of his grandfather.

In his 1972 message to the readers of *Daily Word,* Charles Rickert Fillmore said: "We feel that we are embarked together on this adventurous roadway called 'Life' and that we who understand man's innate spiritual nature can help those who stumble along the way. Also we can share the joyous and exciting discoveries awaiting us around every bend of God's glorious yet mysterious kingdom.''

Rickert Fillmore's daughter Rosemary Fillmore Rhea is director of the radio-television department of Unity School. Two of Charles Fillmore's great-grandchildren are workers at Unity headquarters. Rosemary Fillmore's daughter Rosalind Fillmore Grace is copywriter in the advertising promotion department of the school. Constance Fillmore, the daughter of Charles Rickert Fillmore, is copy editor in the editorial department of Unity School.

The chronological span of Charles Fillmore's life can be appreciated best by those who have a sense of history. When Charles was eleven years old, President Lincoln was assassinated. When Charles passed on in his ninety-fourth year, President Truman was in office.

During his long career Charles was a contemporary of many of the writers whom he admired and quoted. He was a contemporary of Emerson and Longfellow. He was twenty-eight in 1882, the year in which both Emerson and Longfellow died. His admiration of Emerson increased with the years. Many times he would say to his students, ''Anyone who wishes to understand metaphysics should study Emerson.''

A list of the contemporaries whom Charles quoted would include the Brownings, James Russell Lowell, Nathaniel Hawthorne, Carlyle, Bryant, Tennyson. In the 1930s Charles' interest in the latest scientific discoveries led him to quote Sir James Jeans, Robert Millikan, Sir Arthur Eddington, Albert Einstein—contemporaries also, though at this period he was their elder. This wide range of interests indicates an ever-progressive vision throughout his life, a rare gift in this world.

Age has its victories no less renowned than youth. Not to lapse into decrepitude, but with the passing of years to become keener of mind, more flexible, more joyous, more progressive in thought—this is a victory of a much higher order than any victory of youth. Not to be abraded by the frictions of the world—this is a noble victory. Not to be weighted down by the accumulation of years, not to become world-weary—this is to overcome the world. In their description of Charles Fillmore all his friends describe a warm human being with these characteristics.

Charles Fillmore always declared that he did not believe in old age, and he manifested his belief. As a boy he fought death and won. As a man he fought the physical debility resulting from his accident and won through to vigor and health. His teaching regarding health is of profound importance to all those who seek a progressive way of life. He taught that man expressed health, not to enjoy mundane pursuits, but to engage in spiritual enterprise.

His spiritual enterprise bears fruit in the Unity movement. It bore fruit in the inspiration he awakened in his fellow workers. He attracted to himself a group of workers, men and women whose lives he blessed with his vision. Charles and Myrtle Fillmore were creative spiritual artists whose medium was the human heart and soul.

Those who recognize the existence of a divine Plan in the world may also recognize in these events the signs of an advanced soul bringing a spiritual world enterprise to fruition. To use an idiom of the East, Charles Fillmore knew himself to be a member of the ashram of Jesus and he lived and acted accordingly.

Statistics can do no more than hint at the importance of the Unity movement today. The area of Unity Village is slightly more than two square miles. The working force in the village consists of over four hundred and thirty people—executives, Silent Unity workers, office workers, printing plant workers, farm workers, and gardeners. There are about two hundred year-round residents in the village.

In summer, when weekly retreats are in full swing, the motels and cottages are filled with some 250 visitors, week after week. In 1972 over 1,700 visitors came to week-long retreats. During the year, other visitors, who stayed for a day or two, totaled 12,000. The Unity cafeteria feeds all these people with delectable dishes, serving three meals a day throughout the year.

Professional engineers are impressed when they hear that the peak demand of the village is 1,286 kilowatts, or 1,286,000 watts.

Literary experts are astounded at the output of the Unity printing plant. *Daily Word,* the Silent Unity monthly, has 700,000 subscribers, and some 300,000 additional issues are distributed through various sources. The monthly magazine *Unity* has 225,000 subscribers. *Wee Wisdom* has 110,000 subscribers. The Unity publication book list contains over a hundred books and booklets.

Television and radio specialists are amazed to learn that 260 TV stations carry Unity programs. Some 600 radio stations participate in regular Unity programs. A special series entitled *Unity Today* is also broadcast by 70 stations.

Two hundred Unity centers and churches are located throughout the country, with some 400 Unity teachers and ministers.

Silent Unity receives a million requests for prayer in the course of a year. Two hundred thousand of these requests are telephone calls from all parts of the United States, with an admixture of calls from foreign countries. The other 800,000 requests come through letters asking for prayer, and Silent Unity writes a million letters in reply. In addition, 600,000 letters are written in response to questions asked.

Even so, above all the statistical details—the acreage of Unity Village, the numbers of employees, students at retreats, visitors, books, magazines, TV programs, radio programs, Unity centers, churches, teachers, and ministers—above them all is the spiritual afflatus of prayer, which cannot be measured.

Prayer is the breath of Unity. To millions of people Charles Fillmore gave prayer a new and vital meaning, greatly needed in a world which gave little heed to the beauty and practicality of prayer. While the saints and mystics of all ages have always known this beauty and grace, they are the world's few. Nor have they taught the world that there are laws of prayer which can be used spontaneously as well as methodically to heal all manner of disease.

The world needs prayer, practical, healing prayer, now brought to many through Silent Unity, one of the world's noble sanctuaries of prayer. Silent Unity's telephones, open to the world at all hours, its staff of workers who spell each other in a constant vigil day and night —these express the essence and fruitage of prayer.

How shall a man be measured? How shall he be known?

Charles Fillmore gave the world much, but through the immeasurable gift of Silent Unity's continuous, healing prayer to the world he may truly be known.

"By their fruits ye shall know them."

Bibliography

Unity Books and Periodicals

Published by Unity School of Christianity, Unity Village, Mo.

BACH, MARCUS. *The Unity Way of Life,* 1962.

BUTTERWORTH, ERIC. "Charles Fillmore, Prophet of Modern Science," *NEW,* October, November, December 1967; January 1968.

DECKER, JAMES A., ed. *Unity's 70th Anniversary,* 1929.

FILLMORE, CHARLES. *Christian Healing,* 1909.

————. *Talks on Truth,* 1926.

————. *The Twelve Powers of Man,* 1930.

————. *Metaphysical Bible Dictionary,* 1931

————. *Prosperity,* 1936.

————. *Mysteries of Genesis,* 1936.

————. *Jesus Christ Heals,* 1939.

————. *Teach Us to Pray,* 1941. (With Cora Fillmore.)

————. *Mysteries of John,* 1946.

————. *Atom-Smashing Power of Mind,* 1949.

————. *Keep a True Lent,* 1953.

————. *The Revealing Word,* 1959.

FILLMORE, MYRTLE. *Myrtle Fillmore's Healing Letters,* 1936.

FREEMAN, JAMES DILLET. *The Household of Faith,* 1951.

GATLIN, DANA. *The Story of Unity's Fifty Golden Years,* 1939.

Modern Thought, 1889, 1890.

Christian Science Thought, 1891, 1892.

Unity, 1891 through 1972.

Articles, books, and references in this text:

ARNOLD, EDWIN, Sir. *The Light of Asia.* New York: Rand-McNally & Co., 1892.

BAILEY, ALICE. *From Bethlehem to Calvary.* New York: Lucis Publishing Co., 1937.

BRADEN, CHARLES S. *Spirits in Rebellion.* Dallas: Southern Methodist University Press, 1963.

EVANS, WARREN FELT. *Esoteric Christianity and Mental Therapeutics.* Boston: H. H. Carter & Karrick, 1886.

GAZE, HARRY. *Science of Physical Immortality.* New York: R.F. Fenno & Company, 1904

———. *How to Live Forever.* Englewood Cliffs, N.J.: Prentice-Hall Inc., 1954.

HOPKINS, EMMA CURTIS. *Introduction to Scientific Christian Mental Practice.* Cornwall Bridge, Conn.: High Watch Fellowship, 1958.

INGE, W. R. *Christian Mysticism.* Meridian, N.Y.: Living Age Books, 1956.

TOYNBEE, CHARLES. *The Religious Experience of Mankind.* Reviewed by Ninian Smart. *The New York Times Book Review,* February 9, 1969.

TROWARD, THOMAS. *The Law and the Word.* New York: Robert M. McBride & Co., 1925. Currently published by Dodd, Mead & Co.

UNDERHILL, EVELYN. *Mysticism.* Meridian, N.Y.: Living Age Books, 1955.

WATERHOUSE, ELIZABETH, ed. *A Little Book of Life and Death.* London: Methuen & Co., Ltd., 1951.

74 75 76 77 10 9 8 7 6 5 4 3 2 1